Communication Skills

Stepladders to success for the professional

Richard Ellis

intellect™
Bristol, UK
Portland, OR, USA

658 45

ELL.

First Published in Paperback in 2003 in Great Britain by
Intellect Books, PO Box 862, Bristol BS99 1DE, UK

First Published in Paperback in 2003 in USA by
Intellect Books, ISBS, 5804 N.E. Hassalo St, Portland, Oregon 97213-3644, USA

Published in Hardback in 2002 in Great Britain by Intellect Books, Bristol, UK
Published in Hardback in 2002 in USA by Intellect Books, Portland, OR, USA

Consulting Editor: Masoud Yazdani
Copy Editor: Holly Spradling
Production: Robin Beecroft

A catalogue record for this book is available from the British Library

ISBN 1-84150-087-9

Printed and bound in Great Britain by Antony Rowe Ltd, Eastbourne

Contents

Introduction

The ability to communicate is a vital ladder to all career development. Without sufficient communication skills it is possible that there will be little movement upwards (or increasingly these days, sideways). If you are planning one day to develop your own 'career' in self employment then communication skills will be critical to any chances you have of gaining, holding and enlarging your client base. There is considerable evidence to suggest that those who lack communication skills find it difficult to advance their careers. This shouldn't really surprise us if we consider just how much time we spend communicating with our colleagues, managers, clients and customers and how the quality of that communication will affect our relationship with these.

Surveys of what employers are looking for when they recruit graduates suggest that effective communication skills are very high on their list. However, there is some vagueness as to what communication skills actually refers to — that will be addressed in these pages! Many people — you may know some — are effectively blocked in their careers because they are unable to draft that report, make that presentation or sustain that interview. This book is concerned with providing you, the professional, with approaches, techniques, advice to assist you in your communication skills and so unblock barriers to progress in your profession.

The words profession and professional are rather vague; as far as this book is concerned they refer to the work that someone does which requires special training/expertise, for instance accountancy, teaching, medicine, law, surveying, health and safety, personnel, politics? (there's one for an argument!) If your particular profession is not in the above list please don't take offence!

This book is best regarded as a guide like one to the countryside (or the search for that favourite pub!). Dip into it for particular advice on particular issues; for example, how to write that letter of application to go with that CV, browse through it for ideas; it might spark off some thoughts for your next presentation to clients.

As this book is concerned with skills we will take some time to examine how we can develop skills of communication; we'll present some contemporary research on skills acquisition and development (see chapter 2).

Getting up the stepladder

A stepladder is just that — a means by which you can take certain steps to reach your goal e.g. change that light bulb in the hall. In fact that's quite a good metaphor: very often in our careers we will need to 'change light bulbs', get some new ideas, develop brighter ways of communicating, put new sources of energy into our talk and writing, hence this book.

1

Developing your self-esteem and reducing stress

If we feel confident about our communication then this tends to increase our self-esteem and, in turn, our feeling of self-worth. There are very many people who have never developed this sense in themselves and consequently find it very difficult to be assertive and confident in their communication with others. These feelings of inadequacy can increase stress — we bottle up our feelings instead of expressing them, and this can do damage to our health. Enhancing your skills in communication should have real benefits to your health. If you look and sound more confident, people may think you are more confident; this can have beneficial consequences for you.

We cannot promise you that by reading this book and acting on its advice you will immediately experience less stress in your life but it may help. It should certainly encourage you to be a more confident communicator. We very much hope that the experience of reading this text and taking the ideas back to your life and work does increase your feeling of esteem.

Careers today

We make much use of this in the book and so a word of explanation. Some years ago, say before the 1970s, careers meant exactly that: gradual and in some ways quite predictable steps upwards — under factotum, factotum, senior factotum, managing factotum etc. These days there are still careers, one can still move from junior doctor to house officer, registrar and consultant but in many organisations there is now a core and a periphery, the core — these are the essential workers — and those on the edge, the periphery who may be engaged job per job, short-term contract by short-term contract etc. Charles Handy has written of the increasing emergence of the 'portfolio career' where there are a number of distinct strands within it; this he suggests will more and more replace the traditional career of junior to intermediate to senior to retirement.

Professional competence

We will be dealing with these in chapter 2. We are familiar with the word skill. As professionals you will have gained certain skills, you will also be learning through your professional practise of how to use those skills in order that you achieve competence.

The notion of competence has been much written about: it implies knowledge of the what (for instance, the core professional concepts) and knowledge of the how (the ways in which we put these concepts into practice). This implies that what we do is underpinned in some way with concepts of 'theory', in other words our skills are not built up haphazardly; according to the theory of competence we may build up 'theories' of how things 'work' — what is successful, what fails, what could have worked better etc.

Reflective learning

David Kolb in his work in reflective learning suggests that we should move from the experience (that meeting which didn't come off) to reflection (Why not? Was it the agenda, the timing etc?) to thinking about various concepts and theories, i.e. theories about the effect of peer pressure or groupthink (see page 66).

Following this we should move into active experimentation such as 'Let's try this change at the next meeting', and further reflection on the results. (So how did these changes operate?) His model (1971) follows the pattern in Figure 1.1.

In essence then the experience will, if possible, be followed by some kind of reflection. We have to admit that for most of our professional lives it is very difficult to do this; things happen too fast, we cannot take out time to reflect. 'Sorry boss, I'll be late for the meeting, I'm reflecting on that recent memo you sent me'. Such a position is not defensible, it couldn't work. However, we should make an effort to build in some reflection time into our work.

Communicative competence

The notion of communicative competence rests on a similar foundation of theory, reflection and experimentation. It is pretty clear that few of us actually do much of this experimentation and reflection; most of our communication just happens, we are far too busy coping with work, with life, with crises, with computers and troublesome work colleagues. What Kolb suggests is that we should spare a few minutes from our busy lives to reflect on our communication. We should do this to increase our communicative competence (the ability to do and the knowledge of just how we do it). For instance, we should take a few minutes after that meeting to review it, after that presentation to think of how the audience responded; after that interview to see whether we actually covered the ground we had planned. Doing this is a discipline; it requires time to be set aside for it, it is a time management discipline. This books aims to enhance this discipline. It also aims to enhance your knowledge of the various concepts underlying communication. Hymes (1979) has written about this:

> Communication competence refers not only to the ability to perform but also the knowledge of how to perform.

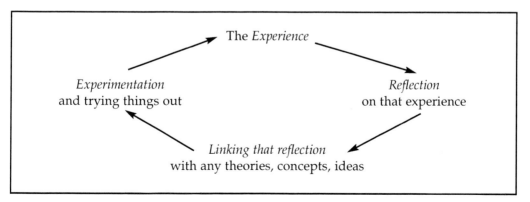

Figure 1.1

It is this ability both to do and to know why one is so doing that, as we saw in professional competence, applies equally strongly to communicative competence.

The reflective practitioner

Kolb's work lies at the heart of the concept of the reflective practitioner. We can define this as thinking/learning as one works, not just repeating mistakes and going over old ground but stretching our intellectual muscles and moving into different patterns of behaviour. This is increasingly favoured in medical education, teacher training and MBA programmes. The use of reflective diaries is increasingly popular. We hear much about lifelong learning and we realise just how impossible it is for us to continuously train. One of the very best forms of ongoing training, CPD (continuous professional development), is based on these notions of appreciating what we do and how we do it. To some extent it is a habit which we should encourage ourselves in; that habit of self-analysis and reflection before we rush off to our next 'performance.'

The learning organisation

The reflective individual lies at the heart of this concept. It has become something of a holy grail; we know it must be there but most of us have never seen one that is a truly learning organisation. The provision of training for all staff cannot guarantee this will happen nor will investment in the latest technology. We have to be able to tap into and mobilise the individual motivation and enthusiasm to do the job better, not to be content with the average, to learn from successes and failure, all of which implies some notion of being reflective.

The concept of a learning organisation needs to be driven and encouraged from the top. Senior staff need to provide an example of learning, of reflective practice and desire for self-development. In the author's experience it is quite rare when companies are drawing up their training plans for senior staff to be encouraged to draw up their own training and development needs. We can recognise the learning organisation if staff can answer yes to these questions:

- Does the appraisal system encourage reflection and learning from experience?
- Is there a recognition that staff will make mistakes and will actually learn from them? (The important thing is not to engage in a blame culture: 'It was all your fault', but to encourage reflection and appraisal so that similar mistakes can be avoided).
- Do staff meetings attempt to encourage this process of reflection and learning or are they forums where people's confidence is lowered and mutual recriminations abound?
- Does the training budget support internal review, building on individual and team success and, are these given proper recognition in the organisation?

This is not an exhaustive list; there may be many other criteria which apply particularly to your place of work.

You might like to pause at this point in your reading to consider the above list and what might be added to it. Or you might like to think about where you work at present. How many of these questions could your manager or HR director answer with a 'Yes'?

So many organisations simply stumble on, repeating mistakes; they spend money on training, but they could never be considered learning organisations. Here's an example from retail.

Every year a large city centre store lays on a Christmas promotion unit; each year they give the management of this to a newly hired graduate to cut his or her teeth on. The staff are hired for the 5 – 6 weeks before Christmas and then paid off. Every year various panics ensue. The staff are thanked for their work and taken out in the last week for coffee and cake on the company, but at no time is any member of that staff asked their opinions as to how the unit might be made to function more effectively. The only review that takes place is that the graduate trainee manager is asked to write a report. The difficulty here is that very few such aspiring managers are going to be very frank about their shortcomings or those of the staff they have attempted to manage. They will not want to present themselves in a poor light. The temptation is to soften the criticisms and lay the blame for various disappointments on lack of floor space, trouble over deliveries, an unexpected surge in demand for this toy or that article.

What we can say is that there is very little learning that goes on either by individuals (they're just part-timers) or by managers (I'll be moving to Lingerie next week) or by the organisation. Many of the problems of this Christmas will occur again next Christmas. If senior staff aren't interested in learning from the past, one can hardly blame the staff for not being motivated to reflect, to analyse and to seek to enhance the standard of work.

Communication and the learning organisation

You may be asking what has all this to do with a book on communication skills? Developing a learning culture has everything to do with communication. This culture will just not happen by itself, it has to be engendered and nurtured. It requires communication through recognition of the individual, effective presentation of the ideals of the learning organisation, sensitive and well conducted appraisals and meetings; it may mean developing a mentoring system for individuals where they can receive one to one assistance (see page 153 for more details) Above all it lies in the communication of values that praises individual learning and the use of initiative; that recognises that the individual member of staff is the most precious asset to any organisation and that the establishment and nurturing of a learning culture requires communication on an organisational, team and individual level of the highest order.

We hope that in reading this book and reflecting on the various concepts of communication that it contains that you too will feel more able and motivated to reflect on your success and failures and by doing so this will enhance your self-awareness of your strengths and deficit areas of communication. This analysis should in turn assist your professional career. In short, the hope is that you will become an individual who learns and who will, because of this, enhance the learning culture of any organisation you decide to join or the one you eventually form!

Efficiency and Effectiveness

We need at this stage to consider the difference between efficiency and effectiveness in communication. We may have a very efficient form of communication, for example e-mail: it is rapid, gets to everyone on the system and is cheap. However, is it effective? Do those receiving it actually take notice of the e-mails?. There is considerable evidence from audits of communication, including those run by the author, that many e-mails are ignored. The sheer deluge of electronic communication is causing acute problems. Many people at work are being swamped with communication, so what looks like efficiency may not be so in practice. To make e-mails more effective we may have to follow them up with phone calls or visits. All the evidence from audits suggests that people find face to face communication by far the most effective form of communication. This evidence shouldn't really surprise us. But effectiveness like this takes up time. We may increasingly have to invest time in our communications, including more face to face talking and listening in order to avoid wholesale wastage of electronic messages. (see page 63)

References

C Handy, *The Future of Work*, Penguin, 1984.

D Hymes, *Communicative Competence*, Penguin,1979.

D Kolb, *Organisational Psychology*, Prentice Hall, 1971.

Further reading

M Pedler, J Burgoyne & T Boydell, *The Learning Company*, McGraw Hill, 1991.

Skills development

This book is concerned with the skills of communication and how these skills are developed. We've already noted that skills should be built on some degree of understanding of theory, the key concepts underlying the communicative competence approach. In this section we explore some methods by which you can maintain and enhance these skills.

Motivation to learn

Before we go on to look at some models of skill development we should say at the start that perhaps the most crucial aspect of any skills acquisition and development is motivation. Just think how much you concentrated on getting that driving licence, how much you wanted to pass that test? Would you have developed the skills of driving (or passing the driving test) if there had not been that motivation to get a licence?

A hunger to gain a skill will enormously help you acquire that skill. The fact that you have bought, or borrowed this book indicates that you have some motivation to develop your communication skills. That's a promising start. You as a professional in training, or embarked on your career, will probably be motivated to enhance your communication skills. If you have regular appraisals of your work you may have gained some impression of your strengths and deficiencies in your communications 'portfolio'.

Communication skills are so many and varied that it is asking a great deal for anyone to be motivated to develop each and every one; yet as you will see in this book although the chapters have been set out according to different categories, i.e. writing, meetings and presentation etc., they are intended to weave together to form a whole. Communication is very much an entity which contains many strands as we shall constantly emphasise throughout this book.

Key factors in learning

We should set out at this stage some basic parameters as to how we adults actually learn. We've already mentioned motivation as a key ingredient. Here are some others:

Learners need to be actively involved with their own learning.

This is a challenge for the author of this book since reading a text is hardly an active involvement. To assist with this various case studies and examples have been included. We hope you will think about these and do some active reflection on them. There will be occasions when we invite you to jot down your ideas, put things into a list, prioritise items etc. Try and do this *before* you read what we suggest, this will encourage you to be an active reader rather than a passive one.

Learning needs to be seen as relevant and significant

This will be come apparent as you read this book, the contents have been developed and designed to assist you as a professional develop your careers.

Learning should be linked, where possible, to existing knowledge and understanding

This poses severe problems for the author since there is no way of being able to gauge where each and every reader's understanding is. We have had to make an estimate of where the majority of readers are. We hope we don't disappoint! We have added to each section a short list of key texts which can take your studies further and deeper.

Learning should be presented in a logical order

What is logical will depend to some extent on the reader's perceptions. We shall see in our chapters on report writing and presentation various ways of logically laying out material for your audience. We have attempted in this text to follow a logical path i.e. from general to particular, from overall concerns of communication to the particulars of specific skills.

Learning should be sufficiently challenging.

You, reader, will have to be the judge of this. Challenge yourself with the various exercises; carefully consider how you could apply the various ideas to your workplace.

Learning should be reflected on

We stress the need to reflect on your learning as in our discussion of the Kolb model on page 3. The book is intended to assist you with linking theory with practice. Charles Handy has said that there is nothing so practical as a good theory, we would subscribe to this view.

The learning of skills needs to be accompanied by feedback on performance.

Practising a skill without gaining feedback is very often a waste of time unless that is you are prepared to give yourself feedback

How did I do today? Not bad

The trouble with this kind of self developed feedback is that we are often just too close to be objective. As an example: we can take a box of 500 golf balls and proceed to drive them at the range; this will provide us with plenty of exercise and not a little frustration mingled with odd moments of exhilaration. What we need is someone to provide us with feedback — but not too much. If your coach keeps piling up the feedback like this:

Hands up a little; shoulders down a little; left hand round; knees bent more; head slight to one side; cock the wrists more; keep head still; lower left shoulder

you will suffer from overload and become confused! Feedback like this is almost useless; there's too much of it and it's coming too rapidly to be of much help. It needs to be specific and well timed. We cover various ways of giving and receiving feedback and we recommend that you look for a coach (see page 153) who will be prepared to offer you useful and reliable feedback on your communication.

Skills acquisition

The model in Figure 2.1 depicts how we acquire skills and starts from that time when we arrive as complete novices to when we perform so fluently that we no longer realise what we are doing. This model based on the work of several skills developers (Landy 1989) can be applied to taking driving lessons.

When we sit in the car for the first time with our instructor we are in a state of unconscious incompetence; it doesn't take very long however — just long enough for us to narrowly miss that car — for us to move into the second state — conscious incompetence. This is the arousal stage. This state may last some time. Eventually we gain skills and pass our test. We slowly move into the unconsciously competence stage. It is only when we are attempting to give a beginner some lessons do we slip back into that conscious competence stage. The final stage is one which few of us reach. As far as driving is concerned then it is only when we decide to take the Advanced Driving Test where we will be asked to provide a one hour running commentary on our driving do we move fully into the conscious competence stage. This 'final stage' is not depicted on this model.

Using this book

We hope that by reading this book and thinking about the various issues raised that your consciousness will be raised and that you will be more able to link theory and practice together.

Let us see how this model of skill acquisition might be applied to the development of communication skills.

When we take driving lessons we usually start from cold, whereas when we pick

To From	Unconscious incompetence	Conscious incompetence	Conscious competence	Unconscious competence
Unconscious incompetence		Arousal		
Conscious incompetence			Instruction	
Conscious competence				Practice
Unconscious competence				Use

Figure 2.1

up a book on communications or attend a course on the subject we have a stock of experiences to draw upon. However, there are bound to be certain aspects of communication which we are not very familiar with. For instance report writing. This might be something that you just do; you normally plough on without much awareness of what a report is; you have never received much feedback. The ones that you normally write are more like extended memos but as no one has done much to help you stick to it (Unconscious incompetence). However, your manager suggests that you attend a one day effective report writing course. Your awareness is raised and you return consciously incompetent. You now need feedback, advice and some coaching before you can put the lessons of the day into practice and move to conscious competence.

We trust that this book will assist you in developing your skills. In the final chapter we outline recommendations as to how you can maintain and further enhance your conscious competence to become a more advanced communicator!

References

F. Landy, *The Psychology of Work Behaviour*, 4th edition, Belmont Wadsworth, 1989.

Further reading

S Covey, *The Seven Habits of Highly Effective People*, Simon & Schuster, 1992.

D. Statt, *The Psychology of Work*, Macmillan, 1994.

Interpersonal skills

This term covers a wide range of communication skills. It is useful in that it implies a sense of completeness in communication — all the various components being brought together. We say someone is interpersonally skilful and by that we mean that he or she can do more than just listen or can present well, or can negotiate well; there is this sense of an embracing ability, and within their communication skill many strands can be recognised.

We say someone is a good driver and by that we mean that he or she is not just able to use the brakes well, steer effectively or change gear without crunching, it implies a sense in which all these sub skills are brought together smoothly and effectively.

We have placed this discussion of interpersonal skills here to serve as a bridge between the various strands of communication which we will examine, such as listening techniques, use of non-verbal communication, telephoning, assertiveness, negotiation, and presentation skills. We have described these skills in various parts of the book but we shall argue that professionals need these days to be effective in a range of skills if they are to maintain and sustain positive relations with clients, customers, colleagues and managers. No doubt you have come across someone who was outstanding in one area of communication but less so in others. This is not good enough these days: we don't all have to be star performers in the various sub skills but we should strive for a measure of competence in all of them. With the increase in electronic forms of communication, it can be argued that inter-personal skills — those used face-to-face — are even more important.

There has been a good deal of research into the development of these various sub skills. One aspect that has emerged is that at some point in the development of the various sub skills they do all have to be brought together. We can stand practising cocking the wrists, holding the left arm straight and bending the knees through the golf swing but sooner or later we will have to hit that ball off the mat and hope to send it high into the air. Let's face it the golfer is judged ultimately by results — did he or she hit that ball near (or in) the hole and not by the beauty of the left arm movements, the gracious way that the wrists were uncocked and the follow through executed!

We can perhaps think of someone who shows a high level of skill in one area of communication, such as their ability to write a well structured and concise report and their complete inability to present it with the same clarity and conciseness at a meeting of colleagues.

Think now for a moment of someone who you would nominate as being interpersonally skilled not just in one area of communication but across a broad range, it could be a colleague, a client, a friend etc. What is it that this person does in terms of his or her communication? How does he/she behave? What mix of communication skills does this person possess that would cause you to make such a nomination? Think of situations where you have seen him or her communicate. How many sub skills were brought together in the communication with others?

You might have, as part of your selection, felt that this person:

- Possesses a wide range of communication skills; he or she is not deficient in any one area as in our above example of the excellent report writer but lousy presenter. There is a sense of completeness in the communication.
- Mixes the various communication skills well, blends them, i.e. he/she are not just good listeners, but manage to ask interesting questions and then when it comes to presenting ideas it is done succinctly and clearly. There are plenty of people who can perform one or two of these activities but who would find it very difficult to combine all three.
- Shows awareness of the great importance of non-verbal communication — gesture, tone and tune of voice, eye contact etc. and has developed good cue judging skills, i.e. he or she can 'read' the non-verbal leakage of others. This refers to those non-verbal signs that say 'I'm puzzled' or 'I'm bored' or 'I quite like you.'

There is evidence from many authorities in this field that some 50% – 80% of interpersonal communication comes through the non-verbal and paralinguistic (tone, tune of the voice) channels.

- Has an ability to do all this, to read the situation carefully and then react accordingly. They are similar — using our previous example — to good drivers who sense the road conditions and gauge the use of gears and brakes so as to be able to drive safely even in the most tricky conditions.
- Can cope with a wide range of situations; his or her interpersonal skill is not limited to one setting, i.e. effective as presenters at formal meetings and not at all competent in informal settings, one to one meetings for instance. They have a wide repertoire of communication skills, and although they may not shine in some situations they can at least be reasonably competent in any of them.
- Can get themselves out of communication holes; they do this by altering their strategy to suit the conditions that they are faced with. (see pages 147 – 152)
- Take great care to remedy obvious defects in their communications 'portfolio' so that it doesn't interfere with their work or diminishes their interpersonal effectiveness.

Can you see yourself in any of these descriptions?

We shall now examine each of these separate strands of interpersonal communication. Although they are dealt with separately they do mesh together and should do so. You may want to develop certain strengths in areas which correspond with the demands of your work, but we do recommend that you aim to become as interpersonally skillful as possible — an all rounder who will impress by this ability to cover all the key areas of communication.

Further reading

M. Argyle, *The Psychology of Interpersonal Behaviour*, Penguin, 1983.

P. Burnard, *Communication Skills Guide*, Arnold, 1992.

G. Burton & R Dimbleby, *Between Ourselves*, Arnold, 1996.

E. Goffman, *The Presentation of Self in Everyday Life*, Penguin, 1971.

Your audience

In order to communicate we need an audience — communication is not a solo activity, unless you are make a recording of your 'performance' to play at a later date to others, or keeping a diary! One of the hallmarks of successful communication is tied up with the notion of being appropriate — that is providing the right kind of communication to match the right kind of audience. You've probably heard this kind of remark:

Well what a thing to say in the circumstances?
Not a bad speech but not in front of that lot?
Well it would be OK as an e-mail but this is going to the Board?

What these statements have in common is that they all signify a lack of appropriacy — the communication didn't fit the bill; it wasn't up to what was expected, and it should have been more carefully tuned to the needs of the audience. A communication is only successful if the audience thinks it so. This is one of the hallmarks of successful communication.

Think carefully for a moment of the implications of such a statement. It implies that no matter how much we take a pride in our communication if that has little or no positive effect on the audience, and by positive we mean:

It makes them take notice
It encourages them to read further, listen more
It triggers some questions
It makes them laugh, cry, chuckle, think, wonder, etc.

then our communication cannot be said to be successful. This may sound a little harsh but if we think it through you will see that it is true. There's that presenter on the stage; she's obviously enjoying the talk and thinks she's doing a great job, but ask some of the audience afterwards and their impressions are very different. 'Dead boring!' 'Right over our heads'. This doesn't mean that the audience have to like the communication, they may disagree with it but it has to have an impact on them; it should make them at least take notice and keep them awake.

Communication implies a mutuality, a reciprocation of sending and receiving. James Joyce the Irish poet once said: 'Somewhere between my reading aloud the poem and you listening to it, the poem is born.' Somewhere between your communicating and the audience's listening is the communication!

Information you need prior to communicating

In order then for our communication to be successful in these terms we have to know what our audience will be. This sounds easy but in practice can be very difficult to achieve. Sometimes we do know pretty well who the audience will be. We know that it is Joe who's coming next for the interview, we know that it is Aunt Betty who will read the letter we are struggling with; we can safely assume that it will be an inspector of taxes who will scrutinise our arithmetic on the tax form.

In other situations we cannot be so certain. When we are invited to give a talk we are not able to seek out each and every member of the audience to ascertain precisely what are their attitudes, their interests, their likely reaction to our jokes and stories etc.

This is just not possible. However what we can do is try to put ourselves in the position of our audience, to try to imagine what we might feel when presented with the communication we plan to deliver.

Although this process is valuable there's more we could do. We can and should try to obtain intelligence about the audience. We need answers to a number of questions. These include:

What are their attitudes likely to be?
Audience attitudes towards our communication can range from the highly positive to the very negative. We shall see in chapter 11 on presentation that it can be very dangerous to form assumptions as to your audience's likely predisposition. It is particularly dangerous to assume that they will be friendly and receptive to your message, you can hope so but you cannot guarantee it!

What will they know about your subject?
It is vital to try and tease out some information on this. You will need this if you are going to be able to make a stab at pitching the material at a reasonable level so that you don't either bore them to sleep or go right over their heads and confuse them. It would be very helpful to discover what, if anything, they have had in the way of your subject before, i.e. have they had anything similar on a recent programme, have they ever commissioned a similar report in the past or received a similar presentation?

What is the make-up of this audience?
It will be useful to have information on the size of the audience (particularly important if you are to make an oral presentation); their age range, gender balance; proportion of overseas visitors; non English first language users; familiarity with technical terms; where most of them come from (take care with those Welsh jokes!)

These questions need to be asked and answered before the communication takes place. Where you may ask is all this information to come from? Here are some possible sources:

Organisers of talks and conferences
Publishers and editors of journals etc.
Secretaries of local societies
Chambers of commerce and Local enterprise councils
Federation of Small Business local branches
Colleagues and friends who have already addressed similar groups.

As we have mentioned you will never have complete intelligence about your audience but you should make every effort to push for as much information as you need. We will be saying more on this in the section on giving a presentation, pages 81 – 98.

Post-communication feedback

While it is vital to find out what your audience will need before you start it is also very useful to open up a channel after the communication has taken place. We all need feedback on our communication. We saw in chapter 1 when we were examining the idea of a learning organisation that opening up channels of feedback with managers, colleagues and clients was very important in order that there could be reflections on what we had done and what we could improve. It is essential for an aspiring communicator to be sensitive to the reactions of his/her audience. How do we achieve this feedback? Here are a few ideas for you to consider:

- Put a brief feedback sheet at the back of that report/document and encourage your reader to complete it
- Put out an evaluation sheet to your audience (or a selection of them) after your talk, course etc.
- Put down REVIEW in your agenda and, for example, elicit ideas from your committee on the way you chair these sessions
- Above all be sensitive to the various forms of non-verbal leakage from your audience; be as cue conscious for this as possible.
- Build in time for reflection.

One of the problems facing you will be fatigue setting in amongst all audiences, the fatigue of completing yet more questionnaires etc. However it is worthwhile trying to get some real quality evaluation; if you explain why it is needed and you make the collection as efficient as possible then you should be able to overcome much of this fatigue.

Asking those questions before you communicate and obtaining some kind of feedback after you communicate will enormously assist your confidence and the likelihood of your being successful. It is certainly worth the effort.

Further reading

G Burton & R Dimbleby, *Between Ourselves*, Arnold, 1996.

Listening and interviewing

Introduction

Throughout this book we will come across listening and its importance in communication. We shall see in chapter 6 just how crucial it is in being interviewed, at handling questions when presenting to groups and the importance of active listening when we occupy the chair or participate constructively at meetings. We have linked this with interviewing because the two are so interdependent. By interviewing we refer to one to one meetings, face-to-face or over the phone, ordinary meetings, panel interviews and those done via video conferencing.

Listening is an activity which is so crucial in all our communication that it deserves this section to itself. Managers in various surveys have put down listening as their predominant activity with some 45% of their working week being devoted to it! You might at this stage like to consider just how much of your time at work is spent listening to others whether this be on the telephone, at meetings, or informal chats. You may be in for a surprise when you've added it all up.

Those of you who have attended time management courses will probably have tried to keep some kind of log of your work activities and divided these up into various categories. Did you include listening in your list? The time spent listening seems to slip by mostly unnoticed, unremarked and uncosted.

You might now, as a result of reading this, like to do an audit of your listening to calculate just how many minutes of a typical day you are spending at it? It could amount to over a third, even on some days, a half. Mobile phones with their incessant demands have added to many people's listening load. Auditing in this way will give you an idea of the quantity of listening, we now need to move to consider the actual quality of listening; they may not be one and the same thing!

Active listening

We can be listening — certainly to any casual observer it would appear that we are in fact doing so — but we are actually doodling, daydreaming, thinking extraneous thoughts, particularly as X walks by our desk...... What we may well have been doing is hearing rather than listening. You may be familiar with the phrase, 'I hear what you're saying'. This often implies that the person is not really paying much attention — it's just being absorbed without much, if any, intention to act on the words or ideas concerned. It can be interpreted as a dismissive phrase which reduces the importance of the other's contribution., i.e. 'I hear it but now let me have my say — what you've said has passed over (into thin air!).

Hearing is normally defined as a fairly passive process, the material just comes in and is absorbed as in the following examples: 'I can hear the birds', 'We can hear the trains running particularly when there's a westerly wind'; 'Sometimes you can hear the planes taking off'; 'We heard various noises but didn't think to mention it'. These are all examples of hearing as a passive activity. Sometimes we start off by hearing and end up with listening, for example, that mobile phone call in the train compartment; all you're conscious of to start with is how annoying that voice is breaking into your concentration and how much you wish that person would not speak so loudly. Then you begin to pick up the odd word and phrase which you recognise; that person's talking to a client of yours; you bend forward pretending to read your papers but intent on picking up every syllable. Now you're listening, really listening. This example shows how we might separate out the passive hearing and the more active listening.

The concept of the 'Active Listener' (Anderson & Lynch 1988) has gained currency. Successful listening (as opposed to the more passive hearing) is to do with actively processing the incoming information and doing some work — hence the term active. The authors define this as:

> The active listener is one who weighs up incoming information to ensure that it is coherent with information that is already available, whether that established information is derived from general background knowledge or specific visual data or from what has been previously been said.

Then they suggest that:

> When incoming information is not consistent with already established information, the listener has to do some extra work. First he/she must recognise that the information is inadequate or inconsistent, and secondly, he/she must identify where the inadequacy/inconsistency lies, and thirdly, do something about it — such as checking, asking questions etc.

Notice the three distinct stages: recognition that there is a gap, identification of where there is a gap and moving to repair that gap. We must therefore as active listeners be prepared to ask ourselves questions such as: 'Why am I listening to this?' 'What would I like to gain from this?' 'How does what I'm listening to equate with what I've just been given?' etc. Posing questions such as these helps to ensure that we remain active and do not slump into being passive. Trying to follow these three stages explains why active listening is such hard work and why to do it well makes us feel quite drained at the end. Being an active listener is crucial when it comes to conducing interviews, as we shall see later.

Barriers to active listening

It's all very well to talk about the need to be an active listener and it sounds all fine in theory but we know that in reality it is so much easier to be a passive listener — the active variety requires much more effort. If we can think of those barriers which reduce our active listening then we may be in a better position to counter these and develop more active listening habits.

Try now and list on a piece of paper what you would consider to be those main barriers at your work that make listening so difficult, then compare them with ours.

Motivation to listen

Let's face it if we are really interested in something then we will listen; think of those lottery numbers over the radio, or the scores from that football match! If you manage others then you will soon be familiar with the sheer number of accounts, explanations, complaints, evasions, anecdotes, accusations, worries and even compliments you will be asked to listen to. It is no wonder that so many managers learn to tune out and indulge in passive listening, as in:

'Yes,.....fine,.....um,.....yes,.....I see,.....well,.....'

We all have to wage a personal war against such switched off listening. We'll look at ways of doing this later in this section.

Attention span

Research into listening to lecturers (Bligh 1997) shows that most of us can maintain quite high levels of listening for about 15 – 20 minutes. After this it becomes increasingly more difficult. We will see on pages 90 – 91 that presenters should be aware of listening fatigue from their audiences. Apart from such events as talks and lectures any sustained period of concentrated listening can be very tiring. It is far better to try to listen in short concentrated bursts than in long stretches; give yourself a break from listening to refresh you. When carrying out interviews do not try and cram too many into one part of the day, allow sufficient breaks for you to catch your thoughts, have a coffee, stretch your legs (and your ears!).

Familiarity with the material

The more familiar we are with material the more likely we are not to listen actively or intently to it. This is a problem with any kind of interviewing and it explains why it is very dangerous to second guess what the other person is saying. It is a very common fault and most likely to occur when we can predict more or less what the other person is going to say. Most of us are pretty good at making such predictions but we do have to watch out since there will come a time when we predict wrongly and we will miss something important, as for example in this scene where the admin. assistant is providing travel details to her manager:

'It's pretty much as before
'Oh yes' (*The manager replies*)
'Yes pretty much the same, similar times, same airline.
'Fine' (*The manager says and stops listening because he's heard all this before, these travel briefings from the assistant have a monotonous regularity*)

18

'You'll be landing at the north end this time'.
'Right *(he says, busy with papers and not noticing the importance of what is being said!)*

Next day as this manager waits impatiently at the south terminal of Gatwick airport for the contact he wonders why there's been this delay. He just didn't listen to the message; the fact that all the time he's been doing this journey and he ended up at the south terminal made him a passive listener, he'd heard it all before and therefore failed to listen to the one vital alteration in the plans.

Attitudes

We have already seen how attitudes may affect the way we perceive incoming information. Our attitudes tend to distort this information: if we approve of the person we may listen more intently; if we disapprove then we may tend to close information out. This has tremendous implications for us as interviewers, and it can also affect the way we take notice, or fail to do so during telephone calls and meetings.

'Hello Sue, it's me, Tim'
'Yes hello *('God what a bore how can I get him off the line?')*
'I've got an idea for you'
'Yes... good.....' *(said without enthusiasm)*
'You remember we were talking about those shares.....'
'Yes....shares...um *(Sue's tuned out from this conversation just because she finds Tim boring, long-winded with a thin high whining voice which puts her off taking him seriously, a pity since it later turned out that this was a hot tip!)*

If we want to be successful listeners we have to *postpone* our judgement until we've actually listened intently to what is being said. There is a way we can do this by remembering SIER rather than SEIR, that is Sense, then Interpret and leave the Evaluation until much later. (R stands for response which normally comes after we've listened!). The tendency is that we Sense and then immediately make an Evaluation based often on surface features such as accent, attractiveness, height, colour of eyes etc. This, as you can imagine, can be very dangerous. We will note the importance of this improved model of listening when we examine interview skills later.

Environmental considerations

There's no doubt that if we are uncomfortable, too hot, too cold, sitting on a very hard chair, suffering from failed air conditioning, draughts from loosely fitted windows and sunlight pouring through broken blinds then this will certainly affect our ability to listen.

Having catalogued the barriers we now consider what we can do to enhance our listening ability.

Enhancing our listening

Before reading on you might like to consider what strategies you have made use of, if any, to enhance your listening abilities. Reflect a little on your personal experience. We can offer you the following suggestions:

• Just being aware of the sheer difficulty of listening and noticing the differences between hearing and active listening will take us part of the way.
• Being able to consider active listening as very much a two-way process, since it depends on both listener and speaker (sender). There has to be some kind of recognised dance step between the two. One of these 'steps' is for us as listeners to keep awake by providing or thinking through short summaries of the input. This forces us to be active in our listening and helps to re-assure the speaker that we are concentrating on what he or she is saying. If we have a very rapid speaker, or if the incoming information is very complex or very dense, then we may have to interrupt the flow in order to ensure we are keeping up, e.g.

Just before you go on Susan can I attempt to summarise what I feel are the key points so far. You've mentioned that the change process hasn't gone that far in hospital administration; you've also registered concerns about the communication of our change programme to staff nurses. Is that a fair recap?

Provided we keep such summaries to a minimum we can not only help ourselves as listeners but stimulate the speaker to continue and to remember key facts. We'll see the value of this technique when we examine negotiating skills on pages 57 – 61.
• We can as listeners ask questions and by doing so we again re-assure the speaker that we are motivated and listening. There is always a danger that our questions will disturb the other person, knock him or her off course and disrupt their train of thought, however if we don't ask questions then we are likely to slip into the passive listener role and perhaps give the impression that we are not that concerned.

Asking questions to improve our listening

The skill in asking questions is to try and build the others' responses so we gain more information, not knock them down so we get less; you can hear both kinds in interviews with politicians!

There is a variety of questions we might ask. It is important for us as listeners to be able to recognise these in order to select the most appropriate for the task at hand. When we are interviewing such appreciation of the various forms of question can be crucial to our success. Briefly we can list these as:

Open

This is where we as listeners are interested in gaining the widest possible range of responses from the other person or interviewee. We cannot tell what kind of response we will get from such a question, which is why we call it open. It serves as a probe to loosen up the flow of ideas, break the log jam and encourage the other person/s to talk.

Can you tell me about your recent experience with ..?
How do you feel about ....?

Closed

This is the kind of question that leads almost inevitably to a 'yes' or 'no' answer. It is used to establish facts and check on details — to be used sparingly. In any interview these facts should be obvious from the CV/application form.

Did you go before university?
Was that the first time you'd worked outside the UK?

Inexperienced interviewers can easily get stuck with closed questions, the interview does not then move onto a deeper, more probing level.

Clarification

Used to clarify information. In all our listening, whether at an interview or not, such questions are the hallmark of an active listener. If only our manager friend had asked a clarification question about his forthcoming trip to Gatwick airport he would have been spared a great deal of trouble and stress. Here are two examples:

Can I just ask you to explain this in more detail? I'm not certain I've fully grasped it.
Is that's always the case? Are there exceptions?

Expansion

This type of question is employed to stimulate the other person to take his or her ideas forward, to provide further material via illustrations, examples etc. Such questions are useful in opening and sustaining any conversation; they are used to stimulate the other person to talk and to continue talking.

I see, could you give me a recent example of how that happened?

Leading

It is important to avoid asking these questions in an interview.

By leading we mean that from the form of the question and the tone of voice used it is very easy to spot where the questioner wants us to go — we are in fact being gently (or not so gently) led! It's the kind of question that defence lawyers are trained to spot and if they smell them will spring to their feet and ask the judge to intervene.

Had you ever thought of stealing these goods before?

My lord I object.
Objection sustained.
Thank you my lord.

It is reasonably easy to spot the obvious leading questions, such as:

> Surely you don't believe in taking the easy way out?
> I'm right in thinking that you'd support management in this decision?
> You're not wanting to challenge this view are you?

It is much more difficult to spot those subtle leading questions which come about more as a result of the way the conversation or interview is framed, by this we refer to the settings, expectations and power relationships between the individuals, such as manager and subordinate and how these might be expressed. In any job selection interview candidates are out to impress the panel. They will be carefully tuning in to the right and appropriate messages as they perceive them. They may well not agree with these messages but they will think it is wise to play safe and agree with the organisation's mindset and the expectations, as in:

> Would you describe your approach to managing teams as participatory?
> (*Thinks: 'I'd better agree and sound keen!'*) Yes very much so.

> Would you want to involve staff in decision making?
> (*Thinks: 'I'd better say "Yes", it's the expected response after all!'*) Yes I certainly would want to do that.

It doesn't exactly take a genius to work out what the 'expected' answer to these questions would be.

We therefore need to phrase questions so that there is no leading element.

Before you read on, just how would you re-phrase those two questions?

Would these be more neutral and less leading?

> How would you describe your approach to managing teams?
> What is your view about staff's involvement in decision making?

Such a re-phrasing doesn't eliminate all elements of leading but it certainly helps to reduce it.

Making use of behaviour questions in interviews.

We hope by using these questions to be able to elicit specific behaviours that the candidate actually used in the past (or claims to have used!). This is one predictor of future behaviour. The use of hypothetical questions such as:

> *What would you do if...?*

provides you with answers that candidates think would be acceptable — the ideal solution and may not actually reflect any actual past behaviour.

Candidates in job selection interviews will often think up answers which will 'please' rather than speak openly and honestly about what they really think and believe. When planning these questions be sure to think of the particular duties that the candidate would be performing. For instance:

- Describe a time when you were faced with a problem which tested your coping skills in. What did you do?
- Give us an example when you felt you were able to build motivation in your colleagues.
- We've talked about goal setting. Tell us about a time when you set such a goal in the past and your success in reaching it.
- Have you ever had to handle conflict in a team. Tell us what you did and what you learnt from that.
- How did you manage change in your last job? What might you have done differently?
- Describe a time when you made a mistake that illustrates your need for further self-development.

The use of such behaviour-based questions is not infallible but you as an interviewer are likely to gain useful and more reliable information than with other questioning techniques. There is some evidence from psychology that it is probably more difficult for candidates to lie when faced with these behaviour type questions since they are so busy trying to think back for instances and examples that they have less time to concoct lies or distort the evidence.

Summary: three key aspects of listening to remember

We all need to listen carefully to what is being said in any work related context, whether that is on the phone, in a meeting or during interviews — selection, appraisal, disciplinary, sales, grievances etc. There are three aspects of listening we should be aware of:

1. We should aim to take in information and try to postpone our judgement of what is being said until we have listened to what the person is saying — right to the end of the utterance.

It is very easy to be unduly influenced by surface features — accent, appearance, manner etc. — and not really listen to what is being said.

It is so easy to estimate, before our speaker has finished, what he/she is saying; to cut across the line of communication with the thought: 'I know all about this'.

We often anticipate what we think the other person is going to say; this can be dangerous! We have to move from listening and then immediately evaluating to listening, trying to interpret and then evaluation.

2. We should aim to acknowledge speakers in a way that invites the communication to continue and develop.

This acknowledgement can take several forms:

- Non-verbal communication; maintaining eye contact, but not staring at the speaker.
- Adopting a comfortable position of not 'over-crowding the listener.
- Adjusting one's position to encourage more confidence and a feeling of being safe.

There is a technique which is called *reflective listening* where we try to reflect back to the speaker what he or she is saying, not in a parrot fashion but reflecting the ideas and especially the mood/emotions of the utterance. This technique is used in social work and counselling. It is a very specialised form of listening and we refer you to texts which will provide you with more information. However, here is an example of the technique being used. An elderly resident is talking to a social worker about how she's had to get used to living as a resident in a nursing home after many years with her family:

> So what with all the fuss and commotion I found it difficult. It was all so different really, not knowing many people, I mean moving there as a stranger so to speak. It was difficult, not easy at first.....missing so much, the family and friends nearby.

> *It wasn't easy then at the beginning?*

> No it wasn't but things improved, got better, made some friends, like Jane in the next room, you know she and I used to know each other way back, funny to meet up again... and after a month or so began to settle a bit more. I suppose you've got to allow that period of time when you first move in, being a newcomer so to speak.

> *You feel more settled then?*

> Yes, though I must say I did miss my old neighbours. Missed them a great deal. Still you've got to face change; there's no point sitting and being depressed.

> *Got to make the best of it.*

> Yes, couldn't stay. Just too much for them, all that work.

The risk in using this technique is that it will appear condescending and vaguely patronising to the listener; it can also lead the speaker to agree with you; the reflective question must truly reflect the speaker's feelings and not be part of the listener's agenda. Had the listener said:

> *Got to make the best of it. The home's better for you isn't it ?*

Here we see how the agenda has been shifted, we are on the listener's ground and away from that of the speaker. She may well think that but she hasn't said it. We must at all times when using this technique take great care not to put words into the speaker's mouths. The skill then of reflection is using it prompt the speaker to continue by tuning into his or her emotions and feelings. Reflective listening is a very useful technique, it is one that most of us have used at one time or another and it can be of great assistance in helping the communication by building a rapport.

3.We should provide limited but encouraging input to the speaker's response which helps to carry his/her and our ideas forward.
Care is needed here. It is all too easy to send wrong signals: '*Uh .... Uh ....*' may appear to us to be exactly that right kind of limited and encouraging input but to our speakers it may seem as though we want them to get on with it and come to the point ('*Oh, do get on with it*').

Our use of questions — those which follow up on a point made by the speaker — can obviously signal to him or her that we are actually keeping up with the information. It is a good idea to check occasionally to see whether our listening is keeping up with the flow of incoming information.

Can I just check with you that...?
Before you go on could I...?

We have to be careful that although we want to turn the interview into a conversation we don't want to keep interrupting the candidate's flow with all these questions.

We can be helped by asking someone to observe during an interview so that we can get some kind of feedback on our performance as listeners.

If our listening improves then it is just possible that others will make more of an effort to listen to us!

References
A. Anderson and G. Brown, *Listening Skills*, Edinburgh: Scottish Education Dept, 1985.

D. Bligh, *What's the use of lectures?* Exeter: Intellect, 1997.

Further reading
P. Burnard, *Learning Human Skills*, Heinemann, 1990.

R. Ellis & A. McClintock, *If You Take My Meaning*, Arnold, 1994.

Being interviewed

We can now draw upon the ideas already outlined, in particular those dealing with listening, interviewing and aspects of non-verbal behaviours. We concentrate here on selection interviewing but the ideas can be applied to other forms such as counselling, appraisal, disciplinary and grievance interviews.

For many people being interviewed is the closest they get to taking part in some magic ritual — it is a process full of secret taboos, strange rituals out of which the result — success or failure, the job or no job — emerges in some mysterious way with little revelation to them, mere spectators.

You may feel this is a somewhat far-fetched description of what selection interviewing is all about; some years ago the author was being interviewed for a job in a Californian bank and as the interview came to an end a young lady from the panel got up, asked permission and began to feel the back of his head for bumps. Phrenology as this is called — finding out about the individual's brain and its power by examination of the lumps — was then all the rage. Graphology, examining the individual's handwriting, is used by a small minority of companies in this country but much more extensively in France. Apart from these examples of 'rituals' there are all the popular theories in the press and magazines which attempt to let the reader in on some of the magic mystery, that unfold the dark secrets of what happens in that interview room:

- Being Interviewed. Your body language counts for more than you think!
- The secrets of interview success!
- Revealed: what personnel staff are really looking for in interviews
- Unlock your hidden personality for that important interview!

This chapter doesn't guarantee to provide you with the success promised by these adverts and articles. What we can offer is a summary of a great deal of current research into interviewing plus the ideas gained from professional interviewers. We will begin with some background material to give you as a candidate some of the current thinking in human relations departments on carrying out interviews. When you come to interview applicants for posts in your organisation you will find this useful but will need to supplement it with more detailed information.

Why interview? The rationale

Charles Goodworth writing in 1985 suggested that the main purpose of a selection interview was:

> To carry out a comprehensive and accurate background investigation, to seek out and verify the facts of achievement and failure.

Some selection professionals would accept that, with some reservations, others would also argue that one of the principal functions of any interview is to see how candidates are able to cope with the stress of being interviewed, how they are able to communicate complex ideas, effectively listen and in general answer the question: why should I be selected and all in 40 minutes!

Another view expressed by personnel professionals is that the interview is there to see if the personal chemistry is right; if there is a fit between the candidate and the organisation. This viewpoint has dangers with its highly subjective approach in that organisations simply find clones of existing staff and fail to take risks with appointments. (He won't really fit in!)

There are other interviewers who genuinely believe that they can in 40 minutes make an assessment of the candidate's intelligence, devotion to duty, honesty, motivation, sense of humour, resourcefulness and personal integrity. It's a very bold claim; we shall suggest that such claims are over ambitious.

Whatever is stated about the selection interview there is one certain thing: it is vital to get it right. The cost of failure may be very high indeed. Not only is it an expensive business but with the The Employment Protection Act and other legislation passed as a result of the UK's membership of the European Union, it is increasingly difficult to 'get rid' of people at work. If the 'wrong' person is selected then it can take a good deal of time and effort and in some cases money, to sort out the problem. Few organisations want to get involved with industrial tribunals! There is also the fact that those who have to be 'removed' because it doesn't work out will go away disgruntled and spread bad news about the organisation that hired them.

Let us now stand back a little and examine the whole interviewing process in terms of sequence of events from the time that the advert is noticed to the time that dreaded envelope with the result is opened. This survey is for both the interviewees and for those who carry out interviews. Increasingly in any professional's life both roles will be undertaken.

Preparation before that interview

Let us start with the vacancy. This is an opportunity to take a good hard look at this and to ask a number of key questions. This is where you need to be assertive and make sure that these questions are in fact answered.

- How does this vacancy look alongside the longer term aspirations of the organisation (i.e. the job might have been applicable in 1985 but now and the future...?)
- If we do decide we need to fill this vacancy do we have someone on the books who can do it?
- If we fill this vacancy then let's have a good look at the job description and see if it needs changing.

We must go through these questions if we are to be able to distinguish which are the *essential* and which are the *desirable* criteria. We need to decide on this before we start advertising for candidates. The drawing up of these criteria lies at the heart of the selection process. It is absolutely vital to think long and hard about this in the interests of both organisation and candidate. What does essential mean? Remember that people can be trained in a skill so that someone who looks promising but who does not have one of the 'essentials' might still be acceptable. Those carrying out selection interviews really must consider these criteria with care.

As an example, consider the situation where a company wishes to employ someone to market their goods in France. The criteria for the job lists fluency in French as essential. Very often organisations will put such criteria down as essential and then wait to see who emerges from the applications and if they can't find anyone with fluent French but someone with conversational French and the right marketing experience then the essential moves into the desirable. After all, an intensive language course can work wonders if the learner is motivated to succeed. We'll see later on how much negotiation and 'trading' there often is in this process of determining exactly what is essential or desirable.

Assuming we have thought about the criteria we can then work on the advertisement. Here we are confronted with the problem that there is a limited space into which a great deal of information has to be put. The advert should be constructed so that:

- It signals the key information
- Clarifies the boundaries of the job
- Entices those who are qualified
- Discourages those who are not.

The advert has to attract the 'best' candidates out of the potentially enormous numbers who will notice the advert. To some extent the selectivity of the advert and the cost can be increased by only advertising in those newspapers and journals which are normally read by persons the organisation wishes to attract.

Great care has to be taken over the wording not only because of those considerations but also because there are certain legal obligations in terms of race, gender, disability, etc. Although at the time of writing the government has not implemented any legislation against ageism, increasingly there will be pressure to avoid those expressions in adverts which stipulate age limits.

What are some of the key words which we as readers of the adverts should pay particular attention to? We could identify these as:

Graduate or equivalent

This phrase may be used to allow those who in the past did not attend university and who have other qualifications to be able to 'enter'. It implies some negotiation in the terms. So it says, 'if you're not a graduate it might not necessarily be the end of your application, we would consider an HND or if you have an excellent track record then we'll turn a blind eye to the whole question of qualifications.

With 5 years experience in a relevant field

Here is a crucial gateway. Does the organisation insist on five years, will three be enough? What is a relevant field? If the post is in IT does the relevant experience have to be within IT or would accountancy or law do? Is this negotiable?

Most selection has to be negotiable: the organisation placing the advert can never be 100% certain that the ideal candidate will emerge. There may have to be some degree of negotiation and compromise in order to achieve the best possible match between the aspirations of the organisation and the reality of the actual market in candidates. Because of the sheer difficulty of framing the advert many organisations now encourage candidates to telephone or e-mail for further information. Web sites will increasingly be used for this purpose. This can be a useful service as it allows would-be candidates to discover more about the nature of the vacancy and allows the organisation to find out more about the caller. This will provide the opportunity for further negotiation as in:

Well how much experience do you have?

We did actually stipulate a minimum of 5 years but we would be prepared to take on someone with less if that candidate's experience was of interest — i.e. especially varied, unusual in its range; was with a competitor etc.

What qualifications do you have?

We did stipulate an Hons 2.1 degree in Physics but here is someone calling who has no degree but an HND with considerable experience in a highly relevant field and can offer fluent French. So?

With that background to the interviewing process in place let us now examine your progress as a potential candidate through this minefield.

The phone call to get yourself an interview

This call is important for both parties. As it is important it deserves having some time and attention spent on it. From the organisation's view it allows for some filtration of applications so that the no hopers are eased out and the promising ones are encouraged to apply. It allows the candidate to find out more about the organisation and perhaps turn a marginal application into a more promising one, so don't rush it. Get yourself prepared, read the relevant advert carefully, underline the key words, such as experience and prepare your case. This after all is part of your interview; if you can sound convincing you may well get called for interview; it is a chance for you to present your case; it may well turn out that you can turn our candidature from 'possible' to a 'probable'.

Prepare then for the likely questions and prepare your replies. Jot down some key facts about yourself; have a copy of your CV in front of you since you certainly don't want to sound vague or uncertain during this call. Your aim must be to get yourself on that possible or probable list so that when you do actually send in your CV your place has been warmed.

Your CV and the application form

When it comes to setting out your CV (Curriculum Vitae — life's story), remember it cannot be a life story. You only have a couple of pages at most, so be very selective. Here are a few pointers for you to think about when you are preparing your CV:

- Avoid producing a general CV. Try and angle it to the organisation you are interested in. Avoid the bland.

- Highlight recent work experience; avoid a long list of duties. Bring out your achievements and any challenges you have encountered and how you have dealt with these. This will be of more interest than O grades gained several years ago. Draw out the essentials that will attract your readers. If there has been a longish gap since you last 'worked' then reflect on your experiences — family, voluntary, community, sporting, overseas etc, to see if these can augment your application. (Transferable skills?)

- Be careful of cliché, management-speak terms: *leading edge; empowerment centred; creative solutions , team player, etc.*

- Avoid lists. If you've been on several courses try and find some kind of thread to link them. You will need to be able to demonstrate that you haven't done a few odd courses or that they have been done to you in some arbitrary way.

- It should be word processed and great care needs to be taken over the structure and layout. Remember this is an exercise in selection. Material must be easy to scan for rapid reading and assimilation of key facts and ideas. It might well be a computer that is doing the initial scanning! To assist:

  - Use shortish lines, wide margins, 11/12 point print, a clear typeface.
  - Avoid overuse of italics, CAPITALS, underlining and bold.
  - Use headings.
  - Replace long paragraphs with bullet points.

Have a close look at these two paragraphs:

A Since August 1996, I have acted as a software engineer to a senior partner in the firm of Slash & Burn, Civil Engineers. Here I have had numerous responsibilities for completing projects centred round new road construction in the Amazon. These responsibilities were for software aimed at budget control of the engineering companies which were subcontracted to the team and who formed part of the project.

B Since August 1996, I have acted as a software engineer to a senior partner in the firm of S. B., Civil Engineers.

Responsibilities included:
- Completing projects centred round new road construction in the Amazon.
- Budget control of engineering companies subcontracted to the team.

A is printed in Helvetica 10 point. It is very dense as a piece of text and reads 'long'. Compare this with B, printed in Palatino 11 point. Much less dense as a text, and it reads more crisply.

- Do think carefully when completing the section on personal interests. This is an opportunity and a very valuable one to show something of you the person. For many people it is the experience that they have gained through their associations outside work that has taught them many 'life skills' and developed their characters. Please don't put down a list of bland interests: TV, music, food. What do these tell about you ? Provide some detail, some interesting 'angles' but avoid fiction and wish fulfilment: hang-gliding, scuba diving and reading Tolstoy. You might be 'found out.' Here is one employer's view of CVs.

Most CVs give too much emphasis on the candidates' factual achievements as described by list of qualifications and posts held than the more indefinable personal elements like initiative and character....I firmly believe personal characteristics are so important in defining the contribution that an individual can make that they outweigh most aspects of experience and training.

(A. Balfour M.D of Insider Group of Companies. Interview in Scotsman newspaper Nov 6th 1995)

This is only one view; you certainly have to put the facts in front of the reader but imagine reading dozens of purely factual CVs one after the other...!

- Check and double check that you haven't made any spelling, punctuation etc. mistakes. Have someone else check it over for you. Eliminate those small errors which may leave a negative impression: BsC for BSc, driving license, (the s form is US English), 'my principle (!) reason for taking this course'. Don't trust spell chekkers! Proof read and have someone to look over the pages just in case you've missed something.

- Don't go too far in getting your CV beautifully typed and bound. By all means make sure that it is a very presentable looking document but to have it produced on gold-tinted paper and velum bound might actually reduce your chances. However this advice will depend on the kind of work you are going for. If you're looking to Design/PR for work then you can afford to be a little more 'creative' with your approach. By all means use a heavier paper than normal photocopying material and place a cardboard backing sheet under it before you post it. Try and use a printer which has a reasonable amount of ink left in the cartridge — if it is printed looking rather washed out then it will all but disappear after it's been copied a few times for any selection panel.

Layouts

There are all kinds of layout for a CV. Don't feel you should copy these — treat them as a guide. Experiment and have a look at what others do. Find a style and layout which suits you. Do make sure that your name is easily located on the top of each page in case they all come apart. If you have not had that much work experience, Figure 6.1 is a model to consider. Figure 6.2 is another layout, perhaps more suitable for those with more work experience. Here the educational qualifications become relatively less important and the work that you have done and your achievements becomes of utmost relevance.

When you have finished the drafting have another read of all the material you have on the company you are applying for. Try and see your application from their point of view. Do a SWOT (strengths, weaknesses, opportunities, threats) analysis:

- Have you shown yourself in the best possible light?
- Have you done your best to reduce glaring weaknesses or deficiencies?
- Have you made obvious your strengths?

The personal profile

This is a short paragraph that sums up the essential 'essence' of what you are — it's a snapshot of you for your reader. E.g.

> Working overseas in a number of challenging posts has given me an ability to improvise, make the best of any situation and be increasingly self-reliant. It has sharpened up my communication skills and enabled me to be reasonably fluent in Portuguese and Spanish. I have proved to myself that I can manage my time, plan projects well and yet retain my sense of humour and interest in my work as a forester.

Name
Address Tel/Fax/E-mail
Education & qualifications
Work experience
Skills
Interests
Referees

Figure 6.1

Name
Address
Telephone/Fax/E-mail
Current post/*A profile could be inserted here*
Responsibilities
Achievements
Previous employment/ Achievements
Qualifications & Training
Skills
Interests
Referees

Figure 6.2

The personal profile must enhance your CV and not become something that puts off the reader from the very start. The various 'claims' made should be supported and amplified during the rest of the CV.

CVs and the Web

Increasingly companies will post up vacancies and information about themselves on a Web site. They will encourage applicants to complete a Web site application or log in their CV under specific categories and according to a set template. It is vital that you do accede to their requests; if they say follow this template then follow it carefully. It may well be that they will just ignore any CV or application which does not conform.

Read the information about the company on their Web site carefully, it may provide you with vital clues as to what they are looking for.

Application forms

The key thing to remember is photocopy the form and do all your rough work on the copy. It is essential to respect the form for what it is: a test of your ability to summarise key information into the boxes provided and to stay within these. Avoid then the use of arrows or other markers which indicate that you have not been able to stay within the spaces provided. Make sure that you have:

- Supplied the information they want (e.g. dates of qualifications rather than what you think they should get — a list of qualifications).
- Avoided leaving any box blank — it could appear that you had forgotten it. If it is related to information which does not apply to you than put a clear line through it and write Not Applicable.

- Filled in the box: Any Further Information. Do practise beforehand. This is a golden opportunity to convince your readers that you ought to be interviewed. Make sure that the information you provide in this box is angled to the requirements for the post.

The Supporting Letter and Letter of Application

If so many CVs look the same and so many good candidates write good letters of application then how can you distinguish yourself? You can do this by:
- Making sure that you are angling your application to the precise needs of the vacancy,
- Showing that you can offer something 'extra' because of your previous experience/qualifications/life experience
- Leaving an impression that you are the person who should be interviewed.
- Avoid the cliché phrases:

If the job description indicates that team work skills will be important, avoid writing: *I am very good at teamwork*. Think of something a little more creative. *In my current post I led the team responsible for X and learnt much about Y and Z in so doing, in particular.....*

If there is an indication that working with people skills will be vital then don't fall into the cliché of: *I am good with people* or *I like people.*. Do add some detail, provide examples to back up any general statements.

Structure of the letter

Here is a suggested structure for you to follow:
- Para 1 — Clarify the post/reference No. that you are applying for
- Para 2 — Give your prospective employer a concise statement of just how you see the post you are applying for. This will be based on your interpretation of the job description and any 'research' you have done on the organisation.
- Para 3 — Explain concisely why you feel that you could carry the duties/responsibilities that you have outlined in the previous paragraph.
- Final paragraph — Express your feelings and opinions about the post. This needs to be crisp and to leave the reader with a positive impression of your commitment to the post.

As your CV will be word processed you might like to hand write this letter of support. If you merely send a letter of application and no CV then you would be best advised to word process this as it will normally be longer and more detailed.

If you hand write a letter do:
- Use decent paper — not small size notepaper
- Use black/blue ink (avoid thin biros — remember this letter will probably be photocopied and faint biro, especially light blue, will not show strongly).

Before your interview

So much has been written and talked about on this subject; pick up a magazine at the dentist's and you will probably find an article on interviews:

Be successful at that interview!
10 Important things to remember when you go for interview!
Those 40 seconds that could change your life!

It all makes good copy but is there any sense to it all? Most of you reading this will have had some experience of being interviewed; some of these experiences will have been uncomfortable, painful even — presumably when you failed to get that job you particularly wanted — others will be more pleasurable, memories of where you did achieve success. You could also call a success those occasions when you might have said 'No thanks' to the job after the interview or even during it when you felt it wouldn't have proved your cup of tea. If you as interviewee have this range of memories so do the interviewers: they have the same sense of relief when it's all over and the same trepidation when the candidates arrive.

Let us, for the benefit of both interviewee and interviewer, see what can be done in the actual conduct of the interview so as to make it as effective as possible — effective in finding the most appropriate candidate for the job. It is surely in the interests of both parties to ensure that this happens. As we've mentioned, conducting interviews is an expensive business, there's the time and the opportunity costs of those involved plus all the admin and support costs and travel expenses to be paid, so here's some advice:

Information on the post. This is an obvious point but sometimes in the author's view this information leaves a great deal to be desired. If the organisation wants candidates to be aware of its mission then this should be made clear. It is also important to signal to the candidate where he or she would fit into the framework.

From the interviewee's point of view it is essential to do more than simply rely on this material; you are advised to do as much as possible to supplement this by finding out about the organisation you wish to join. You want to be able to go into that interview with the confidence that you can demonstrate knowledge and the motivation that you can find things out. From printed information, Web sites, annual reports, reference material in libraries, your local chamber of commerce etc., you should be able to get some grasp of the organisation's principal 'business', recent changes in its orientation, status, markets, research and development etc.

The venue for the interview. This may appear to be an obvious point but it is a vital one. It is in the interests of both parties to arrange so that the candidate arrives at the interview without fuss or bother. Even if you are sent detailed information we would always advise that you check the following:

If you are driving to the interview where exactly do you park? This could be crucial, there's nothing more likely to sap your confidence than driving around trying to find a space while the clock ticks on. Likewise, if coming by train how are you to get from the station? Can you rely on there being a taxi ready? Should you order one to meet you? What happens if your train is delayed? Both in your car and on the train have you got a mobile phone and do you have the number to phone so that you can call ahead and warn of late arrival. They might be able to re-arrange the interview schedule if it was a genuine emergency. Check the dress code required — smart casual or formal.

At the interview

Assuming you've arrived on time how can you give of your best in the actual interview? Much of the following advice will apply if the interview is being carried out on a video conference basis. (Just avoid wearing striped clothes!).

The most important consideration is to try and turn the interview from being an interrogation (yes...no....yes) into a conversation where both parties are listening hard and where a genuine exchange of information can take place. We saw the importance of this in our section on open questioning techniques on pages 20 – 21.The more the interview does actually become a conversation the more likely it will be that genuine information will be obtained and time will pass by more rapidly for those doing the interviewing! Woe betide the candidate who bores them and in whose presence the time drags by!

How does this conversation come about? Well both sides need to work at it. The interviewers need to ensure that the reception is as non intimidating as possible and that at the start of the interview they allow for expected and perfectly natural nervousness on the candidate's part. One useful way for the interviewers to judge the environment is for them to place themselves in the position of the candidate. This is a useful exercise since it might point up that fact that the candidate's seat is so low that it prevents him or her from being able to appear assertive and confident, especially if the candidate is short!

How can we then make the interview a conversation? Here is some specific advice for candidates:

- Avoid falling into the yes/no routine.
- Volunteer information, don't wait to be 'squeezed'.

A paucity of response makes it very difficult for the interviewers to establish a rapport with you the candidate. By volunteering information we don't mean you should gush and swamp your listeners. Here is an example of the different ways in which a question can be answered.

> Did you find your last job interesting?
> Yes, in part

This is not a very satisfactory answer, what part of 'in part' was interesting? This is slightly better.

> I certainly enjoyed the contact I had with members.

However, it still falls short of a good answer. Remember in providing a response you are not just giving a series of bits of information, you are trying to make an impression by suggesting the various skills you displayed, the various aspects of your personality etc. Here's another way of answering:

> I certainly enjoyed the contact I had with members, trying to sort out their difficulties and offering advice as to our services. I didn't so much relish the meetings and the general admin chores but they were part of the job. When the new IT systems came in I found that side less of a chore and more of a challenge.

Here the candidate sends out a signal that he or she has been prepared to buckle down to parts of a job which aren't that exciting and also has some familiarity with operating new IT systems. The underlying message could be: Hire me I'm not afraid of change or of hard work!

* *Establish and maintain eye contact with the interviewers*. Several times in this book we note the importance of this. Recent research suggests that eye contact is not only vital for developing our relationship with others but it assists us in the transmission of information.
* *Try and ask questions in the interview*. Questions are a vital part of any conversation. In many interviews the questions are only 'allowed' at the end. This can make it difficult for candidates since they feel they have to ask something, so very often the questions asked are predictable and banal — i.e. they are not real questions and tend to be about 'safe' subjects such as training and career development. We're not saying that you shouldn't ask questions at the end but if we are to develop a conversation then it is important to we should be able to ask questions when it is appropriate. i.e. when we feel we need to ask. Example:

So most of our trainees would move rapidly through a number of departments...
Can I just ask, would there be any choice as to which ones?

This is an entirely fair question to ask in the circumstances and one that if you had to wait until the end of the interview you might well have forgotten what it was you wanted to raise. If you ask questions politely and ask permission to do so, as in

Could I just ask.....?
Would you mind if I raised......?
Before we leave that could I ask if......?

then interviewers will not mind; it's the rude interruptions and taking over the interview from their direction that is not popular!

* *Stop yourself being torpedoed out of the water*. In chapter 12 on presentation we note that it is vital in your preparation to prepare counters to likely objections. This preparation is important for any interviewee. If the purpose of the interview is to

verify and clarify the facts of failure and achievement then we must expect a number of questions which will probe and seek to elicit responses to specific doubts and uncertainties which may flow from a scrutiny of your CV or application form, covering letters and from references.

So prepare counters to your lack of experience, your patchy qualifications, your decision to change jobs so rapidly, that year you took off to go to Australia, that move from engineering to sales.

Despite all your preparations there will inevitably be 'torpedoes' which you should see coming towards you across the interview room, as in:

You say you were responsible for two members of staff, both part-timers?

This question on the surface looks like an obvious attempt to establish the exact nature of your management responsibilities which were not clear enough from your application, or does the question go beyond that? Does it imply some degree of doubt or concern as to how much real management of people experience you've actually had? This 'torpedo' you will need to turn with:

Yes they were part-timers but responsibilities also included building them into a team with other part-timers in the department; we found that this was necessary to increase their sense of belonging and to give them a feeling of ownership in what we were doing.

This answer demonstrates that you were pro-active in your management of the staff and that you do, as stated, have some useful experience of managing staff. Suppose you were faced with this question?

What did you gain from your 5 years experience of the Middle East?

On the surface it seems like a fairly innocent question but behind this could well be a certain nervousness and unease as to the relevance and usefulness of your time in Saudi Arabia for the organisation. You will need to answer in such a way that the relevance of your experience actually comes through and you do not leave the impression of someone who went out there just for a change, good money and opportunities for travel.

After your interview

Remember if you fail the interview it is important to obtain some kind of feedback on where you went wrong. Many organisations these days will undertake to supply you with information, usually over the phone. Take every advantage of this. It may be that you have been rejected for reasons totally unconnected with your interview performance — they had a better internal candidate for instance, however, there may be clues from this feedback which could be very useful for re-tuning your communication style.

We were looking for someone a little more geared to selling.
(*Did you speak up enough; were you assertive enough?*)
We felt you were more answering your own questions than the ones put to you
(*Did you actually listen to the questions?*)
The interview panel were not entirely convinced as to your ability to manage the team
(*Did you provide enough evidence — examples and the like? Were the answers too general?*)

No one particularly enjoys being interviewed although it can and should be a stimulating experience. Use your interpersonal skills as we have advocated but above all prepare, prepare as carefully and thoroughly as you would for any examination.

References

C.T. Goodworth, *Effective Interviewing*, Business Books, 1985.

Follow-up reading

M. Argyle, *The Psychology of Interpersonal Behaviour*, Penguin, 1987.
H. Dowding and S Boyce, *Getting the Job You Want*, Ward Lock, 1985.

That favourite — the telephone!

Introduction

The telephone is such an obvious, ordinary and totally familiar instrument for communication that we scarcely give it a second glance or thought.

The person who answers the phone is very often at the sharpest end of the company/organisation. His or her voice, manner and style will be crucial in determining whether or not the person calling will have a favourable or unfavourable impression of that organisation.

We have placed it immediately after listening and interviewing since many of the ideas contained in that last section will certainly apply to our use of the telephone.

Factors in successful telephoning

As we have previously noted on pages 12 – 13, research into interpersonal skills suggests that between 55 – 85% of communication comes through the non-verbal and paralinguistic aspects. We cannot see much of the non-verbal communication — the facial expression, stance and gestures, that is until video phones become more common, but we can pick up the paralinguistic features of the caller or receiver, these are concerned with:

Warmth of tone: welcoming and friendly to cool, cold and abrupt.
Pace: fluent and assured to hesitant, slow and halting
Inflexion: rise and fall of vocal tune, interestingly varied to flat, dull and monotonous
Volume: assertive and reasonable to over strong and uncomfortably loud, or by contrast, inaudible and fading to a whisper.

These paralinguistic features are important in carrying the message: the words may be forgotten but the impression lingers and it is the impression that we take away as callers or receivers. This impression can be crucial when it comes to preliminary interviews as we saw on pages 26 – 27 or when we are trying to sell to or influence that other person.

You will probably remember the coldness of a particular voice on the phone and perhaps your associations and impressions about the organisation behind that voice — a hotel, an airline, a travel shop, etc. will be coloured by that poor aural experience. Likewise when you have been received by a warm, friendly and lively voice, more positive impressions will remain.

We should therefore give some time to thinking about our telephone technique — our manner, our style. Here are a few suggestions for you to think about. If you do not think that they apply to you then there may well to a colleague who would appreciate some tactful support in his or her telephone manner.

Timing the call

We need to ensure that when we phone it is an appropriate time for the call. We do not want to break into the other's concentration, intrude into their thinking, acting, preparing or interviewing unless the matter is very urgent. If we are selling then we have to be particularly careful about our choice of time. We need to make use of our negotiation skills as we outline them in chapter 7. As callers, we may need to negotiate an appropriate time for our call on the lines of:

Hello, this X calling. Is this a convenient time to call? I could phone back...

If we negotiate a time when the other party is free we are more likely to get focused, attentive and active listening from them. The danger is, unless we do this, that when the call comes their mind is half on something else and we get pretend listening since they are too polite (and not assertive enough) to say.

I'm sorry this doesn't appear to be a convenient time. Could I phone you back later ?

A little give and take — just that little negotiation — between the two parties can make all the difference to the quality of the eventual telephone call. How many times have you wished you had negotiated and had been more assertive with the caller as in:

I wonder if I could you call later, say after 11.00

How much better to do this than to have half of your attention on the call and the other half thinking of that meeting, which is coming up in 10 minutes time. It is vital that if you do agree to call back at 11.00 you do in fact do this and don't forget all about it. This can appear as a negative move to the other party.

There are several other things we can do to improve our telephoning:

- *Planning the call*. Have a list of topics you want to go through. This is a kind of agenda and again allows you to do some negotiating, i.e. what is important for you and what is for the other party.
- *Summarise the key points at the end of the call*. This can help you remember the key ideas and forms a similar purpose to the summarising that should take place at the close of a meeting. It clarifies what both parties understand has been concluded and those points which will need to be taken forward. This summary helps to demonstrate that you are taking the call seriously. We strongly recommend that you make use of a template such as the one in Table 7.1 for recording your calls. If you make use of something like this you stand a much better chance of keeping good records of calls — essential for your sales/marketing activities, than if you rely on scraps of paper or post-its stuck to the phone — these have a nasty habit of falling off and getting lost.
- *Send a fax/e-mail confirmation of these key points*. Use the summary of the telephone call. Such confirmation will impress the other party that you are serious and committed.

Telephone Call Out/In		
<u>Name</u>	<u>Date</u>	<u>Time of call</u>
Position		Organisation
Points arising from call		
Action		To be taken by.
Name of receiver/caller		Passed to

Table 7.1

Time management and telephoning

It may help you to make your calls in blocks. There is some evidence from time management studies that by doing this you get more fluent and generally sharper if you take a run at your calls, rather than spreading them over a longer period. Obviously it is not always possible or even desirable to do this. If you haven't tried this approach we would seriously recommend that you do.

Feedback on your telephone skills

It is important that you receive some feedback on your telephone manner. It would be very useful if one of your colleagues could be in the same office when you are making the call to provide you with some feedback as to how your telephone manner comes across to him or her. Better still phone up that person on an internal office line and ask for some feedback as to how your voice actually sounds down the line.

Taking some time to think about our telephone manner and giving it a polish may prove to be time very well spent. Table 7.2 shows some of the key features about your telephone manner which will influence how others perceive you. You might find it useful to give this checklist to a colleague who can assess and coach you on your telephoning.

As we said at the start of this section, telephoning is such a very basic taken-for-granted skill and yet how many people do you know who do it well, who appear confident and competent on the phone and help make the other party more at ease during the call?

It is through the telephone that professionals will often make their first impressions on their clients; it is essential therefore that you do have a MOT on your telephone

Feature	Comments
Audibility — can you be heard ?	
Clarity — is it easy for the listener to understand you?	
Pace — Is it varied or tending to the monotonous?	
Tune — Does your voice show interest, or is it tending to the flat & dull	
Stress — Do you stress the important words and phrases-so showing commitment/ enthusiasm?	

Other aspects of vocal manner

Introduction/opening — Does it clarify who you are and what you are calling about	
Probing/questioning — Is this done politely yet assertively?	
Clarifying — Is this done tactfully and convincingly?	
Summarising — Is it done well, do you include the most important facts etc.?	
Closing — Do you close politely?	

Other aspects of telephone style

Overall pace

Evidence of attentive listening, etc.

Table 7.2

skills and approach; this may help you eliminate faults and improve your effectiveness as a communicator.

Further reading

M. Kelcher, *Better Communication Skills for Work*, BBC Publications, 1994.

Assertiveness

Assertiveness is a very commonly used term, so often bandied about that there is a danger that it may become too diffuse and loose an expression to be of much use. 'You're not being assertive enough,' might be about as useful as, 'You're not tall enough or slim enough'. Here is a basis for its use and an examination as to why it forms such an important part of any professional's communication. We've placed it here because assertiveness requires those abilities in listening and interpersonal skills we've previously outlined.

Assertiveness is very much based on rights — yours and other people's. It is included in this book since developing one's assertiveness depends very much on one's ability to express these rights, in speech, in text and through appropriate non-verbal communication.

In developing our assertiveness we will often have to be prepared to negotiate our rights to balance these with those of others. We will see in chapter 9 how the concept of win – win (both sides are winners) is very strongly embodied in successful negotiation; assertiveness is very much allied to this since assertive behaviours help to ensure that both parties' rights are safeguarded. There needs to be a balance and to create and sustain this balance in relationships with others requires a good deal of negotiation.

There is, as we will see, a reference to the idea of the 'bottom line' and the 'walk away position' both terms we will examine in the next chapter. Assertiveness requires that degree of confidence in one's dealing with others, confidence in your ability to recognise and respect your bottom line and that of others and having recognised it then to stick with it and not let it go.

A balancing act

We can see the notion of assertiveness as a form of retaining some degree of balance. If we behave aggressively and drive down the other person so that they have a painful bump — and remember just how painful this could be as a child — the other person will often react by doing the same to us. As we will see in the next chapter on negotiation if we drive too hard a bargain it may bring us short-term gains but in the longer run we may suffer from a lack of business from the aggrieved party. So we may get a rough ride on our balance if we try and push too hard and pull up too quickly.

The other side of this balancing act is where we fail to do any pushing at all — remember how as a child that was so annoying, 'O come on push down so I can go up, come on'. If we just let the other party get on with it, so as to speak, then we are what assertive training calls in the passive state, the very opposite of the aggressive. This passive position suggests that the other person has all the rights and we have very few, certainly not enough to bother the other person with. So with both the aggressive and the passive we are very much unbalanced.

Assertiveness is all about finding a means to get things back on the level. It's about protecting one's rights — for information, to be treated decently, not to be harassed or bullied etc. In real life as opposed to children's games it's often not possible to easily locate the balanced position, sometimes we go too far one way or the other. The important thing is to be able to reflect on our experiences when we couldn't get things into balance. It might have been because we misread the situation, or because our so called assertiveness came across as rather aggressive to others. It might have been because we were working in another culture where assertive behaviour as it is carried out in the UK or US might appear over the top and discourteous to our Indian or Japanese guests. They in turn might appear rather passive to us because that is the way in which they deal with strangers in their midst.

Assertiveness training seeks to increase the individual's awareness of this balance and to provide the person with the skills that should assist him or her to find and maintain it. This awareness needs to be married with reflection on our experiences and adjustment where necessary in our style of communication.

Examples of assertive behaviours

Let's now look at a simple example of assertiveness; it is simple but illustrates a number of key points. The situation may be familiar to you. Suppose you are with a party of friends at a restaurant. You order lasagne and it arrives promptly, looks good, but after the first tentative mouthful you realise that is only partially cooked through — the bottom layer is only lukewarm. Here you are on your balance. Push hard and give the waiter a hard bump: 'This is not properly heated through, it's not good enough, could you take it back and make sure it's cooked.' 'That'll roast him', says the customer to his friends.

That's what we can clearly define as the aggressive position. It may have dramatic short-term results but is it going to result in a win – win for anyone? The author as a student used to see many waiters react to this kind of provocation with a deliberate go-slow to that particular table, or something worse!

Then there's the passive customer. The meal comes, after that tentative bite he pulls a face and his dining companions say, 'Everything all right?' 'Yes...fine'. He replies without much conviction. They urge him to complain, No, he says he doesn't want to create a fuss, it's mostly OK and he adds, 'I'm not that hungry'. This is the passive state — my rights are less important than others'. It suggests by that customer's attitude and behaviour that it's not worth communicating his feelings. No one actually benefits, you, as customer, your companions, the waiter, or the restaurant.

Then there's the assertive position. Yes he is going to take action, but his approach is designed to protect his rights — the customer is fully entitled to reasonable quality food for which he is paying — and the rights of the waiter, who after all didn't actually cook the lasagne, not to be embarrassed, humiliated or generally shouted at. So he calls the waiter over and says in a firm but calm voice. 'Excuse me, this lasagne's not been cooked all through. Could you please take it away and warm it, thank you'. The waiter obliges, none of the customer's friends is embarrassed. The assertive position has in this case re-balanced both parties' rights. It has done something else, it has assisted the restaurant with its quality control. If we receive bad service and unacceptable quality goods and service then if we don't complain in an assertive way how will things ever improve?

This is a simple every day example of what we mean by assertive behaviour. We will see that it is fairly closely linked with the adult state in transactional analysis (pages 51 – 57) i.e. the open, grown up, way of communication, as opposed to the aggressive way which parallels the critical Parent state and is centred round the personal and not the problem.

Assertiveness and communication

How does the assertive person communicate? Think of those people you would classify as assertive at work or in their social life. What is it that they do and say which signifies that they are in fact behaving assertively and not passively or aggressively. Try jotting these behaviours down before you read our list.

The assertive person is likely to:

- Look the other party in the eye, not by staring the other person out, which is very typical of the behaviour of the aggressive person, but by having a generally confident degree of eye contact. This is very important when it comes to interviewing and being interviewed.
- Sit or stand in a way that gives off a confident impression, i.e. not slouching or standing erect but in a comfortable but confident posture. This again is important in interviews.
- Speak in an audible fashion. Passive people tend to mumble, that's one very good reason why that are perceived as passive. Aggressive people tend to dominate by letting the whole room know they're there.
- Assertive people often make use of the 'broken record' technique.

This refers to the repetition of your point of view until it is appreciated, until it penetrates through to the consciousness of the person you are communicating to. It's called broken record after the old vinyl record where the needle could easily get stuck on a scratch. Here are some examples of broken record treatment.

> I regret but that won't be possible. We could certainly get it to you by Thursday noon. No that would not be possible. Monday would not be possible. No. As I've said Thursday noon we will deliver it to you. It would be possible to get it to you on the morning of Thursday.

Here is an example of the broken record approach. The point (no delivery before Thursday) is repeated. Unless this is done calmly and tactfully it can come across as rudeness. One should always be most careful not to overpromise and then have to underperform i.e. let down the other party. Broken record can be a most effective assertive strategy, since the persons using it:

- Make clear what it is they want — there's no fudging or ambiguities.
- Make it clear what are the boundaries, the bottom line, the walk away position —

again there's no fudging. Passive people often find themselves being pushed into agreeing to something and then find it very difficult to 'escape'.

Training ourselves to communicate more assertively

We've already looked at how assertive behaviour can be demonstrated in quite ordinary circumstances such as a restaurant. One of the best ways to develop your own assertiveness is in fact to practise these behaviours in such simple everyday situations. Just think now of those times when you could have acted more assertively and perhaps failed to.

Jot down a list of those times and places where you wished you had acted more assertively. Do this before you read on.

You may have listed:
- That boring meeting where the discussion was getting further and further from the agenda. Did you assert your right not to have your time wasted? For further information as to how you, as a participant, can positively influence the direction of a meeting, see pages 71 – 72.
- That time when you were given the small hotel room overlooking the car park when you believed from your telephone call that it was a bigger room overlooking the lake.
- That person who phoned you as you were sitting down to supper and tried to tell wonderful things about the double glazing consultants who just happened to be in your area. Did you act assertively; thank you, but no thanks, and not aggressively — remember these people have to earn a living as well.

We're sure you can add considerably to that list. Start with such situations if you do not feel very assertive or if others have told you that you need to become more so. You can then graduate to the really difficult manager and customers that you should be more assertive with! There's no point striding into your manager's office and acting assertively if you can't send a cold lasagne back to the kitchen!

Seize those moments at work and in your social life where you need to act more assertively. Let the moment pass and it's so much more difficult to act. Your very absence from action indicates a lack of assertiveness and confidence. Assertiveness is like building a set of muscles: start slowly and keep the exercise moving forward. Then when you feel stronger tackle the really difficult situations we've already mentioned.

As you can imagine there's a whole industry out there ready to help you with becoming more assertive: courses, books, on-line training, self-help manuals etc. Our advice is to try and integrate the theory into your workplace; think about those situations where you could be more assertive. Then go for it! And don't go forget to practise out of work hours. Don't be passive when it comes to poor service.

Many organisations have or are working on codes of working practice for all staff, no matter how senior, to abide by. Here is an example taken from a health service trust.

It is in essence a bill of rights to protect people and to encourage them to behave assertively in connection with such agreed rights:

You have a right to be taken seriously — your ideas and suggestions.

You have a right to express your feelings in an open way without being ridiculed, shouted down or harassed.

You have a right to be listened to seriously.

You have a right at work to be yourself and to set your own priorities provided that those are in line with the work of the organisation and its mission statement.

You have a right to say no without feeling guilty unless you are asked to carry out work in line with your job description and which has been agreed between you and your manager, and is reasonable, within your limits and not in breach of health and safety regulations.

You have a right to ask for what you want. It may seldom be possible to grant everyone's wishes because of the restraints of spending but any request will be listened to and taken seriously. Decisions will be fed back to you.

You have a right to say that you do not understand and to ask for clarification without feeling any embarrassment.

You have a right to make mistakes (and it is hoped learn from these) without being unduly blamed or made to feel guilty, provided you did not deliberately ignore regulations, requests, code of practice etc.

You have a right not to assert yourself or to speak up in meetings etc. if this makes you feel uncomfortable.

Do you feel that this code is helpful for those who work in any organisation? Is it a useful and practical set of rights? Do you have something similar where you work? Could you see something on these lines being introduced?

Assertiveness and handling conflict

As we work in our chosen professions (or not so chosen!) we will inevitably come across conflict. When we manage others we will inevitably come across conflict. In our dealing with customers and clients we will also come across conflict.

Conflict is part and parcel of our work; we cannot escape from it. There's no point thinking that our charm and charisma will enable us to sail through without meeting conflict. In fact we would argue that if you haven't created some conflict with colleagues, clients and managers, or those you manage then you probably haven't been as effective as you could have been! You may have ducked out of taking a difficult decision and left it to someone else to pick it up!

The word conflict is so negatively loaded in its modern usage. But conflict can be healthy. We will see in our section on meetings one of the reasons for actually having a meeting is to resolve conflict.

Some time ago the author visited Indonesia, it was the time of the great forest fires. He was told that the forest fires in themselves were not the danger, they could be put out, it was the fire that went down into the deep roots of the trees which would smoulder on for months and possible years and then unexpectedly on the change of the wind would flare up. Conflict which is open and which can be resolved at a meeting, negotiation, conference or one to one interview is not to be feared, it is that lingering conflict which smoulders on which can prove to be so destructive to any organisation.

At the time of writing this chapter the author happened to read an account of a failing school. The head teacher had tried her best to turn the school round, improve morale but according to accounts she was constantly undermined by a simmering conflict in the staff room that lowered morale, poisoned relationships between senior staff and others and even between staff and pupils. In looking back the head realised that she should have taken much more decisive action earlier on to lance that particular boil.

We suggest then that we need to be able to manage conflict, to bring it out in the open and resolve it as far as it possibly can.

Before reading on we would ask you to reflect on those situations where you experienced conflict. How did you handle it? Did your method help resolve it or simply drive in underground? Such questions will often come up at interviews so that it is well worth spending some time thinking about your response.

Strategies for handling conflict

Avoid

If there's no good reason for you to enter into the conflict then don't. Life is too short and there is far too much to do without having to enter into every argument. For example, if you were running an organisation's training course and one of those present disagree with you as to your philosophy of training then unless it really mattered to you or the group, avoid: simply agree to disagree and get on with the job. There are many situations when we are working with colleagues or clients when we should do this, say to ourselves. Is this important to me? Do I have to get into this? In many cases it will be much the better plan to avoid entering into an argument. The way to determine if you should avoid or not is to use the importance test: is this important to me or my work? If it is then you will need to think up a different strategy.

Accommodate

This is a useful approach where the issue causing the conflict is not of any great importance to you so that you can afford to accommodate the other party's wishes. For example, if you were managing someone who particularly wanted to leave work early two days a week in order to complete a course of study, that was what he wanted and this meant that the only way it could be resolved was for you to alter your work schedule then you might perform such an accommodation in order to resolve the potential conflict. The important thing here is that such an accommodation did not compromise your standards, the procedures of the organisation or set up a precedent which could create problems for you later on. If they did then you should not use accommodation as a strategy.

Compromise

This as we will see in the next section on negotiation will result in both parties having to give up something so as to reach agreement. In the previous example there might have had to be a compromise if no accommodation could have found, i.e. that person wanting the time off would have had to agree to come in early two days a week. Compromise involves giving as well as getting, it involves finding some point of balance between what is ideal and what could be achieved in reality. We will see examples of this used as part of a negotiation.

Collaborate

One of the very best ways to resolve conflict is to work with the other party to seek some form of solution to the problem. Again with our earlier example in mind if there had been no accommodation and no compromise then hopefully both parties would have come together to do some collaboration on the lines on 'Well how can we solve this one: you want to have this extra time for your course, we have to staff the office and there's no one who is willing to undertake extra duties even for overtime. What can we do. Do you have any ideas?'

Notice that the language used here is one of problem solving; so many conflicts can be resolved if people get together, round a table and brainstorm a solution. This is where we will find different thinking and problem solving approaches particularly helpful (see page 152).

The non-negotiable

This strategy is only to be used when we have exhausted all other ones or where the issues involved are so serious and of such fundamental importance to us, to our profession and our business, that there can be absolutely no question of avoiding, accommodation, compromise or collaboration. We just have to be very assertive and say NO.

This is the line which we metaphorically draw in the sand over which there can be no trespass. In our situation if following a couple of weeks of taking the two afternoons off for study our friend then decides to take every afternoon away from the office, despite having agreed to the previous two afternoons position, then this is a case where if you were managing the operation you would be advised to draw a line and stick to it. 'Well Harry we did agree that you would only take two afternoons for your course. That is the position and I must ask you to adhere to that.

Many managers, for all kinds of reasons, ignore infringements of agreements and then find it very difficult, if not impossible to redeem the situation. If you have standards, written agreements, undertakings, professional obligations then these must be adhered to unless there are very good reasons for not keeping them. These are non-negotiable as with health and safety standards. One of the great advantages in having standards that the majority of staff, and colleagues buy into is that it makes it so much easier to enforce the non-negotiable. 'There's an agreement which we all drew up so as this is against it in both spirit and act I must ask you to stop your actions'.

These are some of the key strategies to resolve conflict. In essence, we need to move to a problem centred approach where we can deploy our skills of negotiation and collaboration to solve problems and resolve difficulties. There are many conflicts that we need never enter and many others than can be smoothed over with a little accommodation. The test is: how important is this issue? Is it one where I need to make a stand or should I work out a compromise or can I let it go? As long as you are clear as to the issue then you can be clear as to the treatment. There's no need to use the thumbscrew if a little gentle pressure will resolve matters.

One of the ways in which we can improve our assertiveness and our interpersonal skills in general is to make use of the insights provided by TA, transactional analysis, a psychological model developed by Eric Berne. We refer at the end of this section to some key texts where you can find TA as a theory developed more fully.

Transactional analysis

TA assumes that all events, emotions and feelings we have experienced are 'stored' within us and can be re-called as though on a tape. Of immense significance are the 'tapes' from our childhood. We can 'relive' the feelings we had of our childish joy and frustrations, and our 'childish' perceptions of 'parental' behaviour.

The main states in outline

We can observe three distinct 'ego' states; the 'Child', the 'Parent' and the 'Adult '. These are not abstract but actual states that we can observe in human behaviour. They are not to be thought of literally: children can exhibit very adult behaviours, and adults very childlike ones!

- *The Parent*: this state contains the attitudes, feelings and behaviours gathered from external sources, mainly parents or parental/authority figures. The Critical or Controlling Parent is concerned with laying down strict rules, criticising, punishing; the Nurturing Parent is concerned with fostering, supporting and assisting.
- *The Adult*: this state contains those aspects to do with more objective rather than subjective behaviours and thoughts: asking questions, analysing, evaluating, observing, stating, testing etc.
- *The Child*: this state contains all the impulsive behaviours that come naturally to a

'child': joy, trust, love, tears, anger, sulking, hugging, crying, frustration. It is a state full of very strong positive and negative emotions.

TA suggests that:
- When we are acting and thinking and feeling as we observed our parents do, then we are in our Parental state.
- When we are gathering facts, dealing objectively we are in our Adult state.
- When we are feeling and acting like a child, we are in our Child state.
- There is no prior order of merit in these states; the Adult is not necessarily superior to the nurturing Parent or the Child, just very different. The crucial question for us is how are they used and how should they best be used? We do tend to make us of all three states in our daily lives; hence the concept of transactional *analysis.*

In identifying the states, you will notice from the list in Table 7.3 that many of the behaviours under each of the states are opposites. The Parent state has a constructive and destructive side to it. We could show these divisions as:

The OK PARENT	The not OK PARENT
Helping	prejudiced
Rule giving	persecuting
Nurturing	oppressive
Loving	can't let go
Guiding	

Likewise there are 'OK' and 'not OK' kinds of child.

PARENT	ADULT	CHILD
Sample words & phrases		
There, there,	How ? Why? What if?	Can't, won't
It could be worse,	Test it, probability,	Your fault
Come and tell me,	Have you tried ?	Do it for me,
Because I told you		I'm scared
Gestures & postures		
Arm on shoulder,	Level eye contact	Arms folded,
Holding, nodding,	Relaxed posture	Slumped,
Pointing finger,		Curled up
Tapping fingers on		
Tone of voice		
Sneering,	Calm	Teasing, playful
Admonishing		

Table 7.3

TA suggests that it is possible with some practice and training to switch states according to the situation one finds oneself in. TA warns us against being stuck in one state. You may have found this kind of person — the one who is a stuck adult always objective, always unemotional and detached — not much fun to work with. Likewise the permanent adult who can never ease up, finds it difficult to express joy or become caring when the situation demands it.

Transactions

TA suggest that the Critical Parent state can easily trigger off the Child. We should be very careful of using this at work, i.e., when interviewing for instance.

P What's this about *coming in late all the time?*	*P*
A	*A*
C	*C It's not my fault*

Compare this with

P	*P*
A I'd like to discuss some aspects *of your work, for example reports* *of lateness. Have you time now?*	*A Yes, there is a* *good reason for this, let me explain.*
C	*C*

When someone does address us in a critical Parent tone we should try and avoid getting ourselves 'hooked' by moving to the Child. We should be aiming at turning the transaction into the adult – adult.

This will not always succeed; people get too used to using the critical Parent and find it difficult to employ the Adult. But TA suggests that we should make the effort.

Some people have had very little experience of being communicated with in any Adult tone; they may react with some suspicion to begin with, but persevere. There is also the concept of 'Trading Stamps' which in TA applies to those situations where one person uses an Adult tone only to be given a very critical parental communication in return. This may be explained by the fact that the person being spoken to may have had a bad day and a series of negative encounters with that person and decide to 'trade in his or her stamps' as in the following situation:

Could you pass the toast?
Get your own bloody toast!!

You may have traded in some stamps recently!

Before you read on consider the following pieces of dialogue. A manager is speaking to a subordinate. Which state — parent, adult or child — does each illustrate ?

A. Bill. Haven't you finished that report yet. You're taking ages. I've had to ask you several times for it. Could you please let me have it today. Understood ?

B. Bill, could you possibly do me a real favour and let me have that report. I don't like to keep asking you but I'll be in real trouble if I don't have it for tomorrow. Could you?

C. Bill, that deadline for the report is getting close. We have discussed its importance. I'm getting concerned in case we don't get it done on time. Could we get together this morning and aim to sort out the best approach. Bring any material you have in draft form.

A is very much parental in tone. You can almost hear the sharpness of tone behind the phrase: Haven't you finished that report yet? B is on the child lines: pleading and using the child tone: Could you? Do me a real favour, etc. C is on the adult lines: the reason for the meeting is addressed clearly; it's not a personal one.

Strokes

This is of fundamental importance to TA. People need the stimulation of being 'stroked' A stroke is a form of recognition that one person gives to another. According to TA it is the giving and receiving of positive strokes that develop emotionally healthy people with a feeling of confidence in themselves — a general feeling of being OK. This concept is very important for all managers and supervisors to keep in mind — saying thank you to staff for good work done is so important.

There is the thought that we may be giving others 'plastic' strokes, i.e. empty gestures, words and praise, 'Good', 'Fine' etc. We do have to be very careful over this.

Berne, the originator of TA, described transactions as complementary — this is when both speakers are getting the kind of stroking they want from each other. A crossed transaction creates emotional tensions and will lead to strong negative feelings.

Consider this piece of dialogue, notice how the transactions become increasingly crossed.

Manager: Bill, could I see you for a moment later to discuss that report.
Bill: Don't talk to me about that report. I'm fed up with it.
Manager: You may be but you don't seem to be doing much with it!
Bill: Oh really. I don't see anyone rushing to help!
Manager: It's your responsibility. You know that.

The communication is not going anywhere. The speakers are in a crossed transaction. One of the parties needs to uncross the lines and move into the adult and away from the parent and child as in the previous example.

TA and giving/ receiving criticism

One of the ways in which TA can be of use to us is that it can assist during those times when we have to give criticism, for instance, during an appraisal, or receive it as after taking a test. We need to stay in the adult state and not move into the parental, if we do then it is very likely that we will hook the other's child.

Responding to criticism
There are three forms which we need to be able to distinguish:
- Unclear criticism
- Invalid criticism
- Valid criticism.

Let us deal with each of these and examine the strategies that can be useful in dealing with them.

Unclear criticism
It is vital that we gain clarification; the tendency is for us to rush to deny the 'accusation' and retaliate. There's no point in responding unless we are clear as to what is being said. We need to ask:

> What is it that you don't like?
> I don't fully understand the point you're making, could you explain?
> What you're saying is that you think that...... is that it?

When we are clear as to the criticism then we can begin to respond.

Invalid criticism
If we are certain that it is in fact invalid then this is where we need to bring our active listening and assertiveness skills to bear. We need to disagree assertively, to stand our ground and keep firmly in the adult. We may feel angry inside, hurt even, but it could be fatal to our cause if we let our 'child' out. Count to 10, take a deep breath and reply assertively that you do not agree. You might also give a reason for your stance without becoming defensive. E.g:

> I don't accept that criticism, I followed procedures as set out.
> I would like to put forward my point of view as to that criticism...

It is very important that you gain space in which to state your case. Don't be rushed into replying, allow yourself time.

Valid criticism
If we know that the criticism we are being given is legitimate than the best technique, the most grown-up and adult is to admit it. To the criticism 'You made a mistake!' It's best to reply;

> Yes I did.

Say sorry once but don't go on over apologising, that could be your 'Child' speaking. Avoid counter-attacking with:

> OK I made a mistake, but you make them as well — many of them!

It's a good idea to appreciate the other's feelings as in:

> I appreciate you are worried over this......

It is also useful to look to the future, i.e. avoid any repetition of the behaviour, e.g.:

> I'll be more aware of that in the future. I now realise its importance.

We examined the concept of the Learning Organisation on page 5. Being able to admit our mistakes in an open and adult fashion and being able to prevent ourselves from repeating them is one of the hallmarks of such an organisation.

Other aspects

TA can be applied to *whole organisations:* the climate or culture of the company: for instance we may ask is it very hierarchical and very much concerned with rule setting? Does it encourage the 'adult' by the way it seeks to devolve power and responsibility? The adult one will respond favourably to issues relating to personal development and training; the parental one will most likely say no or place barriers in the way and the 'Child' will just have a good time!

We will see later that TA can be applied to *written communication.* Consider the tone of any of the memos that you produce or ones that you are asked to read. E-mail, because of its informal style and the fact that it is often sent in haste (angry haste in many cases), can produce material which can be parental.

TA can be applied to *negotiation* as we will see in the next section. A negotiation is best approached on an adult – adult, win/win basis. When it is seen as parental (do the other side down) then this can encourage 'child' behaviours from the other party. (If that's how they want to play then....)

TA has been found to be of use in many training programmes. Its aim is to make people more *aware* of their transactions and other people's. It seeks to improve the quality of transactions at work and has been extensively used to enhance inter-personal relationships in such diverse settings as prisons, airports, handling appraisal interviews, doctor patient consultations and family counselling.

Further reading

G. Burton G & R. Dimbleby, *Between Ourselves*, Arnold, 1996

R. Ellis R & A McClintock, *If You Take My Meaning*, Arnold, 1994.

T. Harris, *I'm OK You're OK* ,Pan, 1970.

I. Stewart I & V. Jones, *TA Today*, Lifespace Pub, 1991.

Negotiation

To be an effective negotiator will require all your communication skills: active listening, assertiveness and the use of skilful questioning as well as a clear presentation of your case.

We're talking here about influence, how to get others on side. The word negotiation is often associated with the work of trades unions, government officials in international meetings etc. We often fail to recognise that all professionals in the course of their daily work are involved to some extent with negotiation, it's part and parcel of being in a market, of having to sell your skills to people who will want to get the best deal possible from you for your fees.

Negotiation is a creative process, it seeks to solve problems and remove hindrances and get out of impasses. There are plenty of books on negotiation so in this chapter we are examining the key communications components.

The best known phrase associated with negotiation is one we've already come across and that is 'win – win'. It has almost become a cliché but it is a very important factor nevertheless. The implication behind this is that both sides in any negotiation should gain. They may not be able to gain all they want — that's the nature of compromise and bargaining which is the heart of the process of negotiation.

We can see negotiation in the same way as we pictured assertiveness (page 44). Negotiation is that point on the balance where both parties are roughly balanced as far as their needs and outcomes; if one party squeezes the other and drives a very hard bargain then the equilibrium is upset and the other party will, most probably, want to bounce back and get even. This should caution us against that kind of aggressive, smash the other guy approach to negotiation which is based on short-term gains. Increasingly in business we should be seeking to build longer term relationships with people. A one off negotiation may of course be necessary but if we consider for a moment the time and effort it takes to complete most negotiations, then we will take every effort not to have too many to perform.

Transactional analysis applied to negotiation

We already seen how transactional analysis (TA) can be very helpful when we consider negotiation. If both sides are to benefit in this win – win situation then we will need the adult to adult transaction. Remember that as far as TA is concerned it's much more than just the language used, it is the tone, gestures, relevant written work, even the layout of the negotiation room (we'll seat them over at that end of the table by the air cooler!) — all these factors are of crucial importance when it comes to building up a positive relationship with the other party/parties.

If we can achieve a positive communication then there's a good chance that we can solve the problems in the negotiation. We will examine some of the strategies for problem solving (page 152), of being creative, of using lateral thinking etc. We cannot move to this stage unless some degree of goodwill has been achieved in the various stages of negotiation.

Stages of negotiation

As we will mention on pages 69 – 74 in our section on chairing we'll see that it is vital to work out some kind of agenda; this is as important for negotiation as for meetings. An agenda agreed to by both sides provides a platform for the negotiation. It is also a measure of one's determination to do business and be professional in the job; it demonstrates good time management. It is also a negotiation in itself, by agreeing to the agenda you will establish a climate of agreement. When considering the items on your agenda it is useful to place those ones first that will be less contentious, i.e. where agreement is more easily reached (shall we have coffee at 11.00?) and then move onto to the difficulties. Negotiation is all about building trust, removing suspicion and developing a sense of mutual confidence in the other party. Agree what can be agreed and then move on. If you do get stuck move on and return later to the difficulty.

Finding the appropriate tone in your negotiation

We've already mentioned the importance of tone in interpersonal communication. Where the building of trust is so crucial then great care needs to be taken in how we express ourselves during the negotiation. Any signs of the 'Parental': 'I'm telling you what I want', in terms of tone will be counterproductive as far as achieving our goals of a mutually acceptable solution. Negotiation is one area where our 'Child' can easily be 'hooked' and where we have to take every care that it is not and that we stay in the Adult.

If we are to be confident in our negotiations and stay in the 'Adult' we have to know our bottom line, or as it is often described in books on negotiation, our walk away position. If you enter any negotiation, whether it is selling your car or negotiating a mega deal with a customer, it is essential that you have this bottom line firmly in mind. We saw in our section on assertiveness that it is very difficult to be assertive unless you have this line clearly established. If you don't then you may well be pushed into a uncomfortable position by the other party, this can lead to resentment, 'I'll get even over that...'

Negotiation and problem solving

Negotiation is very much about problem solving and being creative, it seeks to unlock what is blocked, it seeks to open up relationships not close them down. It requires very careful listening, all those listening skills and approaches we outlined in chapter 5 will come in very useful. We need to listen to the actual need as expressed rather than the needs we may perceive the other party to have. We should remember that the other party's announced needs may not represent their real wants. This is natural; we may not want to reveal our hand until we have built up some confidence in the other party. We may state that our aims are with reducing prices but our real need is to be completely re-assured as to delivery and reliability of service.

In any negotiation we need to listen most carefully for these deeper and more hidden needs. If the members of staff start talking about earnings, this may be the main issue but behind this may also be concerns with status and the way that they are perceived to be valued, or not, by management. We saw in our analysis of listening that part of this skill lies in the art of asking questions. It is the use of probing, clarifying and open questions that negotiators can get to the heart of the real concerns of the other party. An example of this could be as follows:

Jane Jones is Training Manager with a large insurance and pensions company. She has worked out her training programme for the forthcoming year and is now approaching various training suppliers with a view to secure reasonable contracts for the provision of certain courses. Let's listen to her negotiation with one of these possible suppliers.

> I've asked you to come today to see whether, following your receipt of our training plan, you can work out a programme which will suit us in terms of the depth and coverage of the training, the methods of delivery and the costs. I should make it clear at the outset that I'm talking to two, possibly three, other suppliers. We'll be able to make a decision by the end of the month.

Jane is laying her cards on the table; this is a good way to start a negotiation, (but remember you may not want to do this until you have established a rapport with the other party!). Think how you would feel as one of the representatives from this training company if the information that there were other organisations in the bidding had come out right at the end or that you had found it out from a third party after your negotiation, that would not have been the way to establish a positive rapport between the parties. The representative for the training company responds to Jane's opening…

> We'd be very interested, as we declared in our letter, in supplying your training needs. We'd like to emphasise what we consider to be our particular strengths. Firstly we've already worked with you and the findings from evaluations on our courses were positive.

This is what we call putting your best face forward. It establishes the position and reveals some cards (quality, reliability etc.) which can be played with more force later in the negotiation! Jane replies to this opening shot:

> Thank you, the evaluations have been positive. As you know we are interested in some 30 courses this year for several hundred of staff. In view of this number we'd be looking at some degree of discounting of your prices.

Here we have the first move in the negotiation. The training company responds with:

> Naturally for this kind of order we'd be prepared to offer a discount probably in the order of a 10 per cent reduction on our printed prices.

Jane like any good negotiator never takes the first offered price. She will appreciate that the company hasn't reached its bottom line yet; this is just an opener. She responds:

> Good, however, given the size of the order, we would be expecting a more generous discount than that.

Here we see the negotiation 'dance' beginning; each party circling the other, testing out the others' intentions and bottom lines. The training company responds:

> Well if those 30 days of training are confirmed then we may be prepared to re-examine our discount rate.

Linkage in negotiation

Here we have a very important aspect of all good negotiation, that is linkage, linking one aspect to another. If you do this.......then we'd do that.... This linkage is the way that good agreements are built up, slowly and with each part linked to the other. The training company have clearly expressed a link between any reduction in prices and the possibility of more than their initial 10% discount.

Jane now moves forward. Maintaining a sense of progress in your negotiation is very important.

> Good, I'm sure we can agree to the discount. I'd now like to explore with you the issue of quality, which is, as with price, crucial in our selection process. We'd be most interested to learn what system you'd have in place if you were to get the contract to supply the training, to ensure that all your trainers delivering courses are working to a consistently high standard.

We will see in our chapter on presentation that as we prepare for any talk it is vital that we prepare counters to likely objections. It would be a foolish negotiator in the training company who had not as homework prepared such a counter to a very obvious question on quality.

> We will set up a lead trainer who will have the job of monitoring the performance of colleagues and liaising with you on any issues that may emerge from evaluations of the courses.

Closing the negotiation

We now move on the end of this particular meeting. Jane brings things to a close.

> Well thanks for coming. Let me try and summarise where we've got to. You as a training company would be prepared to deliver 30 days training at a discounted rate of 12.5 per cent from your published prices. The 5 trainers you intend using will all be experienced. You will appoint a lead trainer who will monitor standards and liaise with us. On our

part we will send you 2 weeks in advance of the training programme a full list of trainees; we will supply the training rooms and photocopy the masters that you will send to us. Well when we've met with the two other companies we should be in a position to let you know our final decision by the end of this month. Thank you. Any questions?

Here we are in the crucial final stage of any negotiation — the close. Nothing can be agreed until everything is checked and agreed. All the various elements in the framework need to come together. A summary at the end is essential. This is where, unless we are very careful, there can be a variety of interpretations, e.g.:

> I thought we'd agreed...
> No we said that...
> Oh I must have got the wrong impression, etc.

In too many negotiations parties leave the room without a clear enough understanding of what has been agreed. It is also essential as soon as you return to base to send a memo or e-mail stating your party's understanding of what has been agreed so that the other party can check to see if it agrees with their understanding or not.

We are all involved in negotiating whether we like it or not. It is essential as professionals that we understand and apply the basic principles and go on learning the skills of negotiation as we advance in our careers and have to make decisions which will affect more than just our fee levels.

Further reading

R. Fisher & W. Ury, *Getting to Yes. Negotiation for Agreement*, Houghton Mifflin, 1988.

J.C. Freund, *Smart Negotiations. How to make deals in the real world*, Simon & Schuster, 1992.

Communication in groups

Introduction
So far we have concentrated on communication on a one to one basis, we now move to communicating with groups, these pose special problems and challenges. By groups we mean anything from 2 – 20 people; once we get over the 20 mark we move into presentation skills; this we examine in chapter 12. Let us now take note of the various factors which mark out communication in groups.

Because we are working with a group it may be more difficult to work out the attitudes, expectations, motivations of its members. In a one-to-one, although it may be difficult is usually easier to get 'inside' the other person and tease out what makes him or her 'tick'. It is usually easier to 'read' the non-verbal elements on a one-to-one basis. When we are faced with a number of faces and many different attitudes and expectations, it is a much more difficult task. This is especially true at a panel interview. We certainly can try hard to decode the non-verbal behaviours of all those present but it is difficult. (see pages 36 – 37) There is more communication-verbal and non-verbal-coming at us from a group. Conversely there is more energy required of us in our communication. We may have to 'play' harder.

We can think about one to one communications which are very stressful and difficult as in some interviews and appraisals. However as a general rule communication to a group will require more effort. In a one-to-one we can (but it is not recommended) muddle through a communication, hoping to negotiate and find some compromise, this process is very risky in a group. We shall see on pages 82 – 83 just how important it is to gain as much information as possible about the nature of the group we are to communicate with — their attitudes, and expectations.

The use of warm ups with your groups can be very helpful, even just to elicit names and roles/designations. We can go in for more elaborate ice breakers such as asking each member of the group to talk with his or her neighbour, ask questions about why they have come to the meeting/training session etc. and then report back to the others. You can introduce some interesting dimensions into this by asking people to nominate one like and one dislike.

There is a greater risk of failure with a group communication. This is particularly true of speaking to a group where the risk is so apparent — all those faces turned up looking at you. We hope that all this is not putting you off from communicating with groups. There are some advantages:

It may often be easier to obtain feedback from a group rather than the one person. This is obvious really when you think of it. If after you've carried out a one to one communication and then you ask for some kind of feedback on your performance it may be very difficult for that other person to provide you with kind of criticism. You know how it is — you're sitting with that other person and then he or she asks you, 'Well how did that go?' and then you say, 'It was OK:' Now that is a great deal of help as you can appreciate. With the group when you ask them for any kind of feedback it is a little easier because each member can as it were 'hide' in the anonymity of the group.

It is often a much more efficient way of communicating rather as lectures are an efficient way of getting information to large numbers of students at one sitting. Notice we are saying efficient — we are not making any judgements about effective — that is something else. (Efficient and effective are important distinctions — efficient means doing something right, effective means doing the right thing.)

Let us now move on to some ideas relating to how we can improve out communication within groups. But first of all we should briefly analyse some concepts of group behaviour.

Stages groups go through

Why is that some groups manage to work well and others get stuck and seldom ,if ever, manage to compete their tasks.

This question was formulated in the late 1960s by Tuchman who suggested that groups may pass through a number of stages. In summary he called these:

Forming: that is when the group comes together, gives itself a name and starts to finds its feet.

Storming: this is the time when the groundrules get settled, when the agendas are sorted out, when roles are clarified and the remit, purpose, terms of reference of the group are settled. Storming may occur at the same time as the forming stage.

Norming: This is where the group has settled down to its task or should be.

Performing: The group is working with most participants clear as to what the task is all about and their respective roles within the group.

Adjourning: Here the group's work is completed.

There may be an additional stage, *mourning*, that is a sense of loss after the group has broken up. Unless carefully handled this can create a feeling of disappointment or resentment even unless there is due recognition of the work done by the group and its contribution. Managers and supervisors need to be sensitive to these feelings.

In terms of communication an important aspect for us is the second stage, the storming. This is the point in the life of any group where things can get stuck, and often do. People are often not sure what they should be doing, their role and unsure what the purpose of the group is — the task. Tuchman suggested that if groups fail to go through this very necessary stage of 'conflict' — such as asking these questions and getting answers to them — then the life of the group might well dry and it would not be able to accomplish its goals. It is up to each and every member of a group to see to it that the storming is carried through and not left neglected. We have examined conflict on pages 49 – 50 and stated that conflict can be positive provided that it is brought out into the open and not left to smoulder 'under the table'.

Storming then is about getting conflict on the table where it can be talked through and hopefully resolved. If groups don't have a good storm then they may never be able to resolve the conflict that comes about because members are unsure, unhappy, bewildered and fed up. So, individually, when we are asked to join a group, we should ask these important questions:

Why are we here?
What are we supposed to do?
How are we supposed to do it?
By when are we supposed to do it?

You may well have been in a group which has got stuck. It may well have been because of a failure to storm, to articulate the differences and bringing these disagreements out into the open. We do recommend that you make use of such questions.

Roles we play in groups

We examine in chapter 11 the roles of chairman and minutes taker and also of ourselves as participants in meetings. One researcher, Belbin has spent a great deal of his working life examining the roles that people play in groups. He has sought answers to this question: Why do groups fail despite having clear leadership, clear goals etc? He suggests that successful groups require a mix of team types and that it is only by achieving this mix that groups will flourish. He puts forward the notion that in a group we often play two roles: the first is our professional/technical one, that is fairly obvious; we attend the meeting as lawyer, doctor, accountant, pharmacist etc. But we also bring ourselves, so to speak, we bring our personalities, our intellect, our ways of thinking etc. This is our team role. Belbin has isolated eight of these roles. He provides an extensive self-administered test which enables individuals to discover the role or roles that they most prefer, the ones they could perform if need be and the ones that they would not want to perform unless asked to do so. This is a useful way of looking at these team roles:

- Our preferred
- Our secondary
- The ones we feel uncomfortable in.

This is not the place to go into these roles in depth. As this is a book on communications we will concentrate on what an understanding of these roles can do for our confidence in expressing ourselves within the group. Here is a brief explanation of the main roles. We do recommend that you read Belbin's books on the subject.

The Shaper. The characteristic of this type is that he or she tends to be outgoing, dynamic with a readiness to challenge. The downside of this (the allowable weakness as Belbin puts it) is a certain impatience and irritation with any delay. You can imagine how useful such a shaper is in a group but how difficult it would be with several of them! A shaper's typical remark would be:

> Come on, we've already spent some time on this, we must progress.

This raises quite fundamental issues relating to who should chair meetings, see pages 70 – 71. Shapers often make ineffective chairs. They are so keen to push things along that they do not allow time for questions and discussion.

The Plant, so called because Belbin suggests that we may actively to import such a person to our group. The plant is that person who is full of ideas, highly creative; their allowable weakness is that for much of the group meeting they may not be with us but dreaming up new ideas. Plants may get put off by strong shaper behaviours particularly if that shaper happens to be leader of the group or chair:

> Come along Brian not another of those crazy notions. Let's have something sensible shall we?

The Completer Finisher: that person who attends to the detail, who pays attention to the minutiae. His or her allowable weakness is to worry overmuch about small trifles, but what an asset to any group and how sorely is that person missed!

> Can I just check that we've booked the room and organised the speaker?

There are other team types including the *monitor evaluator* who is good at asking the difficult questions, such as why are were here? What are we doing?

The *chairman*, this is a person who acts calmly, is good at getting people to talk and build consensus. We will see more of this role in our next chapter.

> *You might like to think from the ones we have so far identified where your preferred role would be and where your secondary role would come.*

Belbin's work should help us be more confident in groups. If we can see that as well as bringing our technical, professional expertise with us into the group, we also bring ourselves and our preferred role/s then that should provide us with more confidence to speak out, to question, to play an active part in the life and work of the group of which we are members. It can also be very helpful if you are to chair a meeting as we will see on pages 72 – 74 It can open one's eye to the value of team roles.

The problems of conformity in groups.

The distinguished psychologist Asch spent a good deal of his time investigating the issue of conformity within groups. He noticed how the presence of the group — the peer pressure — caused individuals to change their views according to the prevailing group opinion. You may have noticed this yourself.

> *Think for a moment of a situation — for instance at a meeting where you have wanted to say something but you realise that your views would have been different from those of those sitting round you. Why in retrospect, did you not speak out? Was it because you felt embarrassed, that you might be ridiculed, that your views might give rise to conflict and disagreement etc.*

Asch pin-pointed this problem: he realised through a variety of studies that peer pressure acted like a wave which easily swept across a group reducing the variety of individual opinions to the one 'safe' one.

We will see on pages 72 – 73 how an effective chair can warn off this 'disease' by giving explicit permission for members of the meeting to disagree and take an individual opinion. The chair can also stimulate debate in the way that he or she steers the meeting: stirring up the discussion, inviting minority views, ensuring that these are recognised in the debate and in the minutes. However it is so important that the chair stays neutral and impartial in the actual debate.

Group think

The other researcher we should take note of is Janis, an American psychologist who has studied what he calls Groupthink. He has defined this as:

> What happens when a group of people who respect each others' opinions arrives an a unanimous view, each member is likely to feel that the belief must be true. This reliance on consensus validation tends to replace critical thinking.

The solidarity of the group tends to view criticism as disloyalty. You can image the insidious damage this can do to a group. Members will tend not to speak out in any critical fashion because that will be seen as 'rocking the boat'. This tendency is exactly what the storming part in Tuchman's stages is all about. You may well have been a member of a group where Groupthink had set in. It appears from the research of Janis and others that the longer the group works together the more difficult it becomes for individuals to step out of line and be openly critical. It is a very good idea to have a MOT on your groups so that grievances, niggles and criticism can be thoroughly aired before they are allowed to build up to a major explosion. It is important to take heed of the small shocks so that you are not presented with any nasty surprises.

The cultural dimension to communication in groups.

There are considerable differences between cultures when it comes to communication within groups. For some societies, such as Japan, one needs to remember that many meetings at work are held mainly to ratify ideas and policy and not so much to discuss and argue a case. The storming is very often done in smaller groups and between key individuals. To begin arguing and disagreeing over policy matters in front of the group as might occur in Europe and the US might be seen as bad mannered not only in Japan but in many other societies in the Far East. Many meetings are more ceremonial than business in form and intention: tea may be taken, contracts signed and hands shaken and heads bowed.

Even if the meeting is mainly business we should take great care over such matters as introductions and the use of names. In much of Europe and North America we ask for names or suggest that people write their names — usually first ones — on cards in front of them. In India and much of the Far East such informal introductions could cause offence:

> Your name is Dr Harri?
> 'Yes '
> 'But what do we call you?
> 'Dr Harri is fine?'
> 'Dr Harri — nothing shorter?'
> 'Dr Harri is fine, really'

We do need to be aware of the cultural dynamics, rules and conventions which govern groups in such societies. It requires a keen observation of such niceties; a careful reading of the non-verbal leakage and body gestures. As an outsider one will be allowed to make some errors with respect to conventions but if you want to communicate to influence at meetings and within group situations then you would be very well advised to fine tune your communication style to suit the prevailing cultural norm.

Compliance in groups

The work of Stanley Milgram showed how where there is an element of fear this will affect a group's performance. Individuals will comply with a safe position rather than sticking their necks out. You may be surprised that we talk of fear but in many work groups there is considerable unease and anxiety which can amount to fear. There are increasing numbers of part-time staff, those on contracts, those who are working for agencies on very limited prospects who when in a group, especially one chaired by an employer, manager, the person responsible for their hiring and firing, will often suffer anxiety and stress. Such an atmosphere is hardly conducive to open and free flowing discussion. In order to reduce these fears we have to create a more supportive culture.

At work we also need to ensure that as far as possible those responsible for hiring and firing leave the chairing of meetings where they want ideas to emerge to those less high profile and seen as less threatening by the group.

We now move to consider communication within formal groups such as meetings and to large groups — audiences gathered to hear our presentations.

References

S.E. Asch, 'Studies of independence and conformity', *Psychological Monograph* 70(9) (Whole Issue 416).

M. Belbin, *Managing Teams*, Heinemann, 1984

I.L.Janis, *Victims of Groupthink*, Houghton Mifflin, 1972

S. Milgram, *Obedience to authority*, New York Harper, 1974

B. Tuckman, 'Developmental sequences in small groups', *Psychological Bulletin* No 63

Further Reading

C.B. Handy, *Team Building*, Kogan Page, 1988

Communicating in and out of the Chair

All of you — yes we can safely predict this — will spend time at meetings. If you get really bored sitting there you can add up all the hours per week, per month, per year that you are in or out of the chair. The hours will mount up to something that can be quite frightening.

This chapter is to help you whether you chair meetings, try to participate in them, sit there taking minutes or simply book the rooms, make the tea or do them all!

Key questions to ask before your meeting

Before we enter into the details of these various roles we should set out some preliminary questions, very much on the lines of those we pose on pages 121 – 122 when we look at writing. Again, it's all about being assertive, it's about being brave and asking those questions which demonstrate your assertiveness. It's not about being passive and just getting on with the job. If we have answers to these questions we are likely to be more confident in our role.

• ***Is this meeting necessary?***
I'm sure all of us have attended meetings where we have wondered what the whole thing is about and why we have to sit around aimlessly chatting?

> Is this necessary?
> Yes, its Tuesday, we always have a meeting on Tuesday.
> Yes, I know, but I was just wondering what the point is?
> Of what?
> Well the Tuesday meeting
> You haven't been here long have you?
> No.
> Well every Tuesday we have a meeting to discus what is happening and what has happened. Tuesdays wouldn't be Tuesdays without our meetings. Always get tea and chocolate biscuits. OK now?
> Yes......
> You'll soon get the hang of it. I've been here for years and really look forward to these get-togethers.

You might well have had this kind of experience. We hope you have been assertive and gone on asking this question: is there an alternative to this meeting?

- ***What's the meeting about — its remit?***

It is very difficult for us to be confident at any meeting if we do not know what it is supposed to cover. A good chair should make this absolutely clear, in fact the agenda and other notices from the organiser/convenor/minutes taker should also help clarify the purpose.

- ***What's my role in this meeting?***

We need to be clear as to this if we are to communicate assertively and with confidence. Here are some of the roles you might play at a meeting. Think of the ones which best suit you at the meetings you attend.

- Chair
- Minutes taker
- Representative — i.e. you represent some body of opinion, other members of the staff, a group of clients.
- Delegate. You have been delegated by others to take part, vote etc.
- Panel member.
- An expert called upon to give specialised views
- An observer/consultant who is there to provide advice on the meeting itself, the way it is organised, chaired, the interaction of the various members etc.

Naturally you may be playing more than one of these roles, but whatever combination of role played it is crucial that you don't suffer from role blur — that is not knowing why you're at the meeting. If you're new to the group do make sure that either you are introduced by the chair or you intervene and introduce yourself. Don't just sit there!

- ***What's on the agenda and how can I prepare for it?***

When we have received a satisfactory answer to these questions we can move to active participation.

Auditing your meetings

One of the first stages in seeking to make more effective use of time in meetings, whether you are a member or chairing it, is to determine how much of your working day is spent in meetings and the value of these in getting thing's done! i.e. carrying out an audit. The following is a series of questions to help you identify these issues and begin to determine what can be changed/improved.

In tackling these questions think of a meeting as a gathering of two or more people for a period of 15 minutes or more and which has a purpose.

Note that these might be very informal e.g. the Boss asks you to 'pop in for a moment' (which turns into half-an-hour!) or formal committee meetings with agenda and structured proceedings.

1. How many meetings do you attend/chair each week? Make a list of all meetings with approximate times so you become very aware of the proportion of your time spent each week in meetings.(it is useful to do this with your team)
2. Who attends these meetings? Are they the most appropriate ones?

3. What is the purpose of these meetings? Is there an agenda?
4. Are the meetings well controlled? Does everyone contribute or does one person hog it all?
5. What did the meetings achieve — actions? Passing on information? Getting ideas? Problem-solving?

Action following audit

Having now established what the current situation is for you the next step is to decide what could be changed/improved.

1. *Do you have to meet as regularly as you do at present?* For instance, could that weekly meeting be held as usefully every fortnight? You may need to negotiate with colleagues on this one.
2. *Membership.* Often people get into a meetings attendance habit (it beats working!) We need to be critical of who is involved. Are all the people at the meetings necessary? If two people go from one section could one go instead and report back? Do we have to attend all of a meeting? Could you attend for relevant items only? Do keep a check of who does actually attend your meetings. If you have a representative who never turns up then action should be taken.
3. *Purpose.* Are you always aware of the purpose of the meeting and why you are present? One standard here is to ensure there is an agenda and if it is an informal meeting to clarify at the beginning what it is about (very politely of course!)
4. *Conduct of meetings.* This is often where most time is 'wasted'. As a member of a meeting you can do a lot to improve unsatisfactory meetings by seeking certain standards, e.g.:
   - Do you have the necessary documents in advance? Is there an agenda?
   - Does the meeting start and finish on time? (it is good practice to have a finishing time as well)
   - Is time allocated to items in proportion to their importance?
   - Are people encouraged to contribute?
   - Are you clear at the end of the meeting what action, by whom and by when is required?
   - Are minutes promptly and accurately produced and circulated?
5. *Finally, did the meeting achieve its purpose?* If it did, fine: if not, try to identify the problems and begin to manage them!

Ways in which participants can assist meetings

This process of auditing our meetings and making sure that the key questions as to purpose, remit and our role are answered is something we can all do as participants to enhance our meetings. We can also communicate and contribute by:
- Attending on time
- Reading any background papers and minutes
- Taking action where it says ACTION against our names
- Keeping the chair alerted as to time:
    Excuse me, chair, but if we are to finish by 5.0pm then we'll.....

- Helping to maintain peace and harmony:
    I suggest we take a ten minute cooling off break chairman.
- Assisting with the environment:
    Would it help if we moved the table this way, we could then all see and hear each other?
- Ensuring that everyone is clear as to what is being discussed:
    Chairman I for one would like an explanation of......
- Encouraging the chair to stay on track:
    Chairman I suggest we return to the main problem which is...
- Helping the debate focus by providing a proposal:
    Chairman can I propose that this is circulated to all members with...

Some key skills in chairing

There will be times when we are asked to chair a meeting. Here are some techniques which should help you in this task. One word of advice before we start, don't try and chair a meeting and take minutes, it is just not possible. Chairing should take up every ounce of energy you have, let someone else take the minutes, you will only have time for the odd note to remind you of key points.

Before you read our list of key skills, you might like to think about those times when you've chaired a meeting or those you've witnessed do the chairing. What are the key skills you would put in your list?

1. Encouraging participation from as many as possible

We can use the indirect approach as in:

How do we all feel about this issue ?
Is there any one would like to add a contribution ?

Or we can be more direct and actually ask a participant as in:

Before we go on I would like to hear from Brian on this
Christine how do you feel about this ?
Nick I know you have some experience in this matter, would you like to come in at this point ?
Let's give Theresa a chance to tell us how she views the problem.

2. Paraphrasing

This is where we listen carefully and then check as to whether we have grasped the essence of the point. We might have actually understood the point but we suspect that other members of the meeting are not so sure, hence the paraphrase:

Let me see if I've understood you aright. You mean.........are you saying...?
Let me try and see if I've got the point: you mean........?
Sorry Charley, I see some puzzled faces round the table ......could I try and re-state what I think is the main point here — please come back if you think I've missed anything..

3. Asking for Clarification

It is very important that we should ensure that everyone is clear as to what is being said. We need to chase clarity at all times, particularly if we suspect members round the table may not be clear. E.g.

The examples you've given seem only to concern.....Do they also refer to......? Could you clarify this point ?

4. Asking for a Summary

This is a useful way of controlling a rambling contributor, as in:

Before we move on to your next point, Harry could I ask you to provide a summary for us of the main argument....

5. Providing a Summary

Where there has been a lengthy and complex discussion it is the chair's duty (unless this is delegated to the minutes taker) to provide a summary of the key points. If you are working in small informal groups the chair or minute taker can write up these points on a flip chart. This will provide the group with a running checklist of key points which can form the basis of the final minute.

Before we conclude this item on the agenda, I would like to sum up where I think we've reached in the discussion...
We've spent a good deal of time on this item. Can I briefly summarise before I ask you to come to a decision.
Before we take a vote on this issue here are the key points for you to consider...

6. Ask for Expansion

If you as chair feel that there has not been a wide enough discussion, that the group have somehow got stuck then you can use this technique, as in:

Diane, will you please provide us with an example of what you mean.
Jim, could you please expand on that point a little; give us a little more by way of...........

7. Suggest a Procedure

This is where the group are deadlocked and cannot make progress.

Would it help if we reversed the order on the agenda in view of the fact that....
I suggest that in view of the time we place the remaining items on the agenda for the next meeting.
Things are beginning to get heated....I suggest a 10 min break.

8. *Do a Rapid Survey of Opinion*

Your aim as chair is to build up a consensus so that a decision can be 'owned' by the group.

> *Can I get the feeling of the meeting as to this one....thank you...*

9. *Question Assumptions*

You may feel that the group is not getting 'real' in its debate and that you need to bring them back to the world out there.

> *Your assumption is that there won't be any......to fill the gap. What evidence do you have for this view ?*
> *What evidence is there for thinking that...will increase...?*

10. *Check Your Target*

Discussion can drift, you have to keep a hand on the tiller otherwise you may find yourselves moving away from the items on the agenda.

> *Are we asking the right questions here ....might it be that....?*
> *Are these the only points ....aren't we in danger of missing something important ?*

11. *Put up an 'Aunt Sally'*

This is where you stimulate the group to go deeper in their thinking; you might want to play the devil's advocate if the debate is shallow. (see Different Thinking Hats, page 151)

> *Let us suppose for one moment that...customer...?*
> *Well for the sake of argument don't increase....just...what then ?*

12. *Focus on Action, Implementation and Delegation*

This is very important for you, the group members and particularly for the minutes taker. Far too often people leave a meeting without being clear as to what was decided and who is going to do what and when!

> *Before we end, let's just remind ourselves who is going to carry out the various tasks we've agreed on...the subcommittee will consist of...*
> *and report back before...*
> *The next meeting will have to....deadline must be kept in mind.*
> *We must have the quotations in before....so that we all have a chance to...*

Your role as minutes taker —

Definition

Minutes are a written *summary* of the proceedings of a meeting. They are a summary, not a complete recording of what was said. They normally record:

- The date of the meeting
- The venue of the meeting
- Those present
- Those absent
- The agenda (the items in order)
- A summary of the discussion
- Proposals
- Result of any votes taken and decisions made
- The resolutions/actions
- Responsibilities for those taking on the actions.
- Date of next meeting/s (if any)

Minutes must be an accurate and impartial recording of these aspects.

They must be accurate in the sense that future meetings can build on the actions and decisions made and because they may be used as evidence in a legal setting. (E.g. an industrial tribunal)

They must be impartial — i.e. the minutes taker must not favour one particular side, one argument over others, one member's contributions over another's etc.

Minutes are written in the past tense and all direct speech is turned into reported speech. E.g.

Office communication. (as spoken)

> Chair: Can we start this item on office communication. Thanks. I just want to kick things off and then get a discussion going — well as a start there's a suggestion been put forward that we should investigate some method or methods of prioritising e-mails within this office of ours.

Office communication (as a possible minute)

> The Chairman opened the discussion by stating that a suggestion had been put forward for a priority system to deal with e-mails in the office.

Minutes are a summary of what was said. They are not the full transcript. Leave that for courtroom stenographers.

Your role

You must be confident in what you as a minutes taker are expected to do. Your task is

difficult as it is but is made many more times more so if you are not sure what you are
doing. So do ask; make sure that you have answers to the following questions:

Readership

Who is going to read these minutes? Will the readers be exclusively drawn from those
who attend the meetings? If so, you as minute taker will be able to summarise
proceedings even more tightly. If the minutes will be read by those who have not
attended then you may need to expand some of the discussion. You may need to gloss
some of the jargon and abbreviations.

If the minutes are to be read by a very wide audience then you might like to write a
short report of the meeting rather than minutes. This report could be put up on a notice
board. It should be on a single sheet of A4 and should simply list the decisions/actions.
Passers-by very seldom bother to read copies of minutes pinned up on noticeboards.

What should be recorded?

There may be a house style to assist you in this. Make sure that if you are new to
minutes taking you read examples of previous minutes very carefully. Learn from
these, in particular note the following:
- What kind of numbering system is used?
- How the topic relates to the agenda, e.g.
- Where the actions are placed in the text.
- Whether participants' names are used, or initials/designations?
- How much discussion is recorded? Is it just key points or is there some attempt
  made to record a range of opinions.
- The typeface, pointage (size of letters) and use of CAPS/ bold for headings.

The writing of the minutes

There is a range of techniques for writing minutes. Here is a selection for you to think
about. You may have your own technique which works for you but you might like to
consider one of more of the following:
- Turn your A4 sheet of paper (or better still A3) sideways and divide it into 2
  sections (see Figure 1).

On the left hand jot down your rough notes
using whatever system of 'shorthand' you
use. You might also find it useful to
subdivide your rough notes into two
columns: the *Essential* and the *Possible*.
Under *Essential* you would include:

    key actions
    proposals voted on

Rough notes	**1st Draft**
CL rpt'd rcnt	C.L reported on rev
trvl expns	of travel expenses.
Sggst	He suggested
incr 35p nxt	an increase to
F Yr	37p/m from next
	Financial Year

Figure 1.

Under *Possible*

> elements of the discussion
> background statements etc.

To illustrate this approach here is an extract from a discussion at a meeting. Although it is difficult as you were not part of the proceedings and therefore do not know the situation, make an estimate of what you would put under essential and what under possible. Take a piece of paper and try it.

> Can we turn now to agenda item 3. Travel expenses. I realise that this has been on the agenda before and that members of this committee have strong feelings on the matter. Brian could you kick off.

> I was asked to undertake a review of travel expenses. At present we pay 27 p a mile for all staff working on our business. This rate has now been unchanged for the last 4 years. Several staff have complained to this committee and I promised to undertake this review. I checked with a couple of other companies in our field and in this area and they pay between 30 and 40p per mile. I suggest that staff do have grounds for complaint.

> Thank you Brian. Anyone else like to comment. Susan.

> Chairman I think we should note that petrol and general motoring costs have risen quite rapidly over the last 4 years — when we did the last review of expenses. I'd like to suggest a rise to say 30 p a mile as soon as possible. I know that running my own car that it certainly costs a great deal more. The last servicing bill — things like oil for instance — a tremendous increase, and we know that in the last budget petrol went up...........

> Yes Harry

> Could we not adapt a policy which many organisations have which is to pay more per mile for the first x miles and then a reduced rate thereafter. So that you could have 37p for the first 1000 miles on company business and 29/30p for any subsequent travel.

> Thanks. Any other comments. Brian?

> I think we should go for Harry's suggestion but I'd suggest 40 p for the first 1500 miles because of what Susan pointed out — the big increases in petrol, oil and servicing.

> OK are we getting near a decision? Are we happy to accept Brian's modification of Harry's suggestion? So we agree that 40p per mile will be paid from the beginning of the financial year for the first 1500 miles and thereafter 30p for subsequent mileage on company business. Are we all agreed? Fine thank you. I shall write to all staff informing them of the Board's decision.

We suggest that you could have separated the material as follows:

Essential	Possible
3 Trl expns	
Brian's review of travel expenses	on agenda before
Present rate 27p/m last 4 yrs	strong feelings on mattr
Gen rise in motoring costs	staff complaints to com'te
Unan agreement for rise:	other companies pay 30 – 40p/mile
From start of new Fin Yr	Harry proposed sliding
40p/m for first 1500 miles	scale 37p/m – 1st 1000m
30p/m for following mileage	29/30 further miles
<u>Action</u>: letter from Chair to	Brian's suggestn
all staff	40p 1st 1000 miles 30p for rest

The actual minute could be written as:

3. TRAVEL EXPENSES
Brian reported on his recent review of travel expenses; these had remained unchanged for the past 4 years at 27p per mile. He had checked with other companies in the area and found they were paying more. It was pointed put that general motoring costs had also risen. After discussion it was unanimously agreed that from the start of the next financial year travel expenses would be increased as follows: 40p per mile for the first 1500 miles and 30p for further miles. The chairman would write to all staff to inform them of the changes.

Notice in this version the discussion between Brain and Harry has been considerably summarised. You could easily add more detail and feature much more of the discussion between these two. It all depends what you want to capture in your minute — how far you consider this discussion to be of importance.

It is always very difficult to separate out the essential from the possible. This is where a) the longer you stay as minutes taker with a particular group the more you will appreciate what they regard as essential, and b) the more you can ask for feedback from them (and from the chairman) as to what they require in the minutes, the better able you will be to make your selection.

Other tips for writing your minutes
If you do not have shorthand then make up your own system:
• Use commonly accepted abbreviations, e.g.

Compared with	*cp*
information	*info*
approximately	*approx*

• For rough notes you don't have to use vowels — just use consonants. E.g.

Senior management recommend adoption of marketing plan.

Could be written as:

Sn mngmt rcmnd adpt'n of mrktng pln

- You can also leave out unnecessary words — as follows:

  A simple spreadsheet system could assist trainee auditors
  smpl systm cld asst trinee audtrs

- Remember long words can be shortened, as in:
preliminary	*prelim*
department	*dept*
unnecessary	*unnec*

- Make use of lines, diagrams, mathematical signs etc., e.g.
more than	>
less than	<
rising	↑
falling	↓

What ever system you adopt the key thing to remember is :
- Don't leave it too long before you write up your notes.
- Try and do it the same day.
- The longer you leave it the more difficult it will be to remember.
  those abbreviations, squiggles, arrows, crossings out. etc.

There are a variety of other techniques you might like to consider:

Using a flip chart
For instance with a very small and informal meeting you might like to jot up the main points on a flip chart as the meeting proceeds. You can then get the participants to 'agree' to these points; take away the flip chart papers and work up your minutes from these.

Take brief handwritten minutes and pass photocopies around before the meeting ends.
Again this really can only be used with small informal meetings where the issues are fairly clear cut and there are no lengthy (or heated) discussions to record.

Using a lap top computer
Tap in your minutes as the meeting proceeds (you'll need to be very fast on the keyboard) and either print these off before the meeting closes — in draft — or display

them via a modified OHP to all present. Again this would difficult for more formal and contentious meetings.

So as a minute taker, remember:

1. Be assertive. Ask questions about the minutes and their readership. You are there to help the meeting but you cannot fulfil the role of minutes taker unless you understand and are comfortable with what it is your committee wants of you.
2. Remember you cannot and should not record everything. When you have been reassured as to those key questions then work out a system for yourself that allows you to capture the *essentials* and the *could bes*.
3. Experiment with different ways of recording the information. Try to sit next to an experienced minutes taker before you plunge in solo.
4. Never leave the writing up of your notes for more than a few hours. Try if possible to get a first draft minute written up from your notes before the end of that working day.
5. Check the draft minutes with your chair and other members of the committee/group/panel. Ask for their advice.

Remember the longer you do the minutes for a particular committee the more indispensable you become, so you shouldn't find them unhelpful when it comes to answering your questions! You can always threaten to resign!

Conclusion

So whether you are in the meeting as participant, chair or minutes taker you must know why you're there, be clear as to the purpose of the meeting and your role within it. If you can do this you will get so much more out of your meetings and they won't be such a terrible waste of your time.

Although we may have been critical of meetings in this section we need to remember that they can be of immense benefit to any organisation. We have noted in our section on assertiveness that meetings can help to bring out conflict into the open and under the rules of the meeting and provide a reasonable and courteous way of resolving difficulties. Meetings can also provide protection for people who might otherwise be harassed or put upon in some way. The fact that each member at the meeting is protected by the chair and therefore empowered to have his or her say is a very important benefit that should not be lost. Furthermore in these days where people working alongside each other will send e-mails rather than converse, meetings also perform a very crucial social function by allowing people in any organisation to meet, talk, network, have coffee and just feel part of a team.

Further reading

G. Janner, *Janner on Communication* London: Guild, 1988.

Communicating on your feet

Presenting Yourself to Others

One of the key communication skills for professionals is the ability to present themselves to groups of people whether at a meeting, to a panel for an interview or to a gathering of over a 100 at a sales conference.

One way of looking at presentation skills is to analyse what it is that those who are good at it — the competent presenters — actually do. What is it we ask that marks these people as advanced?

At this point you might like to jot down on a piece of paper those criteria you would select for the advanced presenter. Try to do this before you read any further. Think of those people you have heard give presentations who you thought performed very well. Consider why you thought this and why the reaction of those others in the audience was so positive (that is unless you were the only one who enjoyed it!).

What would go on your list? Here is our analysis; we will start this by following a trail from the reception of an invitation to give a presentation to the completion of the talk and the follow-up.

The invitation to give a presentation

Inexperienced presenters are usually too amazed, flattered or bewildered by the invitation to do much by way of analysis. Their first thoughts are usually: 'My fame is spreading', then after a few minutes of reflection comes the doubts, 'Can I do this'. 'Is the date they want OK for me?' and 'What shall I say in this talk?'

Advanced presenters after reading the invitation put a number of questions to themselves:

- Are there any alternatives to a presentation, a CDROM?
  Is it worthwhile from my/the organisation's point of view?
- If yes, am I the right person to give it?
- Is this the appropriate time to give it?
- Is the title fixed? Can it be altered?

Only after asking these questions and analysing the answers will the advanced presenter start thinking about accepting and preparing for the talk. This reflection as to whether to accept or not is not being arrogant, it is just a sensible attitude to adopt. If you are in a professional career you will be busy so is this a sensible use of your time?

There are very sound reasons for this initial scrutiny: presentations are expensive in terms of time, it is not only the direct costs of your preparation of the materials and the going out and giving the talk plus your travel time etc., but also the opportunity costs i.e. what else you could have been doing if you hadn't been spending your time on all that? We will come up against the very same questions when we look at report writing on pages 128 – 130.

Analysing and clarifying the remit

For advanced presenters, usually as a result of bitter experience, now begins the task of analysing the request. Inexperienced presenters are more or less content to accept the title and remit in the invitation, as in:

> We would like you to speak to...on...at...
> We would be grateful if the talk could be...and if you could concentrate on...
> Thank you very much for giving your time for this.

This is not nearly enough information for the advanced presenter. He/she writes, faxes, e-mails, phones, better still goes to meet the organiser/convenor face-to-face-all this in order to seek answers to a number of key questions:

Expectations: what do the organisers actually want? Is there some hidden agenda here? Is the title of the talk meaningful? Would it be better to change the title, or add to it?

Negotiations: the more experienced you are as a presenter the more you should be able to enter into negotiations over the talk. This advice applies equally to invitations to appear on radio or TV. The inexperienced speaker will seldom, if ever, try to negotiate the terms of the talk. The fact is that most talks are negotiable; the initial remit may well be open to some movement. The aspects that can be negotiated include:

- The title
- The areas to be covered
- The depth of coverage
- Any particular angle to be taken
- The duration of the talk
- The type of visuals to be used
- The timing and nature of any breaks (refreshments)
- Introductions
- Handouts and their printing/distribution
- The environment — you may not be able to alter the venue (but do try if it appears to be unsuitable); you may well be able to alter the arrangement of seats, tables, lecterns, display boards, screens and flip charts/boards.

Other aspects to be negotiated could include fees/travel expenses if you are empowered to do this and if such a negotiation is ethical.

Attitudes: it is always difficult to judge the attitudes of an audience but the advanced presenter has all his or her antennae up and ready to detect any signs. A little bit of empathy can be very helpful. By trying to put himself/herself in the position of the members of that audience it is possible to get a little under their collective skins. The inexperienced presenter can easily misread the signs and, taking the indications to be favourable, enter the hall expecting a positive welcome. This can lead to a nasty fall: the so-called positive audience becomes much less so as the talk goes on. This can turn into a truly horrid experience and in some cases may put that person off public speaking for years.

The competent presenter has probably been caught this way before and is very sensitive to audience attitudes. Such a presenter realises that in any audience there will be some positive members, perhaps a few very much so, the bulk neutral, waiting to be convinced and, in some settings, a number who are negative with the odd one, two or three quite hostile to the subject and perhaps also to the presenter.

One of the first lessons to be learned is that no one presentation, no matter how brilliant and how charismatic the speaker, can hope to turn those negative members of the audience in the presenter's favour. There will usually be a residue who will not budge in their attitudes one inch or one millimetre.

Advanced presenters aim to counter likely objections by the way they deliver their talk and by the skill by which they marshal the arguments and display the facts. We noted the importance of this when we looked at being interviewed on pages 36 – 38. We'll supply examples of this later in this section.

Detailed preparation

Novice presenters attempt to write down the whole speech, even including 'Good morning ladies and gentlemen'. They produce several sides of closely drafted text, each line filled, with very little space left.

Speech

Good morning. I would very much
like in this address to examine with
you certain aspects of the development
of new software systems to handle
the particular problems that we
all witnessed in the last few years.
These problems seem to have centred
round particular difficulties...

Advanced presenters have evolved their own style of notes but never fill the page with text; they know that to carry this up to the podium, lectern, or rest it on their knees is asking for trouble. They appreciate that presentation is all about making contact with the audience, keeping this contact during the talk and using the questions, answers and after the talk coffee break to extend this contact. Such contact can not be generated if all the time the presenter has to scrutinise the text head bent down and voice muffled by the papers.

However our advanced presenters know that on occasions — such as when the press may be there, or where the subject material is risky in legal terms or when they are operating in a second language — then a fullish text is called for. This, however, will be prepared as a speech text and not just printed out line by line from the word processor.

To achieve suitable speech notes our advanced presenter does a great deal of preliminary drafting — brainstorming ideas, listing themes, jotting down key words and linking them into categories. Then after this has been done — keeping the remit for the talk firmly in mind — the speech notes are produced. At this point he or she may just check back with the person who issued the invitation just to double check on the remit. So many speakers get the bit between their teeth and after a few hours of preparation forget about the actual remit and head off on their own. It is very easily done!

Notes for your talk

There are very many ways of organising speech notes; it is very much a personal preference. All we can do here is to outline those which we have found to be useful. Here is an example of preparation taken from the author's personal acquaintance.

The speaker is a transport consultant who has been asked to give a talk to local government officers in his area. He has tried many different ways of organising speech notes. He has come up with the following arrangements:

He uses heavy paper (so that it doesn't shake around in a nervous hand!) and writes key phrases on it with a black felt tip pen or word processor in bold 14 point print. (Please avoid water-based pens. The author witnessed the scene where the chairman knocked over a glass of water and reduced the speaker's notes to an unreadable sea of ink!). He takes care to space out these phrases using the centre of the page. This is important because he wants to be able to focus as he glances down at his notes. Notice how much he uses abbreviated forms so that there is a minimum of reading and a maximum of scanning. These phrases are there to trigger a memory of what has already been prepared. These notes would be suitable for a short (10 – 15 min) talk where the speaker already has a good deal of knowledge and therefore can rely on such skeletal notes.

Transport in cities — Options for C21st

Cars must be controlled

Different licences — diff purposes

Singapore experim't

Devlopm'ts in computis'd signalling

Money generated from licences/fines put back into local system, Dutch systems — Amsterdam

Bus lanes nec for faster + reliable trspt, Edinburgh initiative. Cost benefit analysis — details

This is only one way of putting down notes for a talk; it must be emphasised that there is no one perfect way of doing it. You will, as your experience of giving presentations grows, develop a system that works for you. We do strongly advise that you do experiment and that you don't get hooked on to one way of writing notes.

Some presenters swear by cards in the hand; they have found this method to be one that works for them. You can buy packs of such 6 x 4 inch cards from any stationers and they can be very useful The same advice applies as before — write in bold and in the centre of the card so that you don't have to peer. They are particularly useful when you have to walk about while you are presenting, as when you want to move from a lectern to point to a screen or where it would not look right to be holding pieces of paper as at an informal gathering such as a colleague's leaving do, a vote of thanks, and that most difficult of all tasks, a best man's speech!

Whether we use cards or sheets of paper the key point to remember is that the notes must be of use to you. If you are unhappy with your notes then this will add to your sense of nervousness. Your notes must support, not distract you. If you feel that kind of speech note illustrated above would just be too brief for you then you can always expand to suit. The following example shows how the basic skeleton of notes can be amplified — the lines have still been laid out for rapid reading.

These notes are more detailed and yet retain the essence of simplicity and conciseness. Whatever you do, don't pack too much into your notes — they are and must always be a distillation of your preparation, not a text of all that you have prepared.

Transport in cities — Options for C21st

Cars must be controlled; UK one of most rapid
    car growths in Dev World   *slide 1*

Different licences — diff purposes
    Time to move from one overall lic. Singapore experim't

5

Full lic — v expensive — all week
    off peak lic — suit retired / freelancers special weekend only lic
Electron systems now v sophist'd works by recog
    lic plates, auto debit bank tech'ly now possible

Devlopm'ts in computis'd signalling   *slide 2*

12

Money generated from licences / fines
    put back into local system
Dutch systems — Amsterdam   *slide 3*

Bus lanes nec for faster + reliable trspt
    Edinburgh initiative   *slide 4*

20

Cost benefit analysis — details   *slide 5*
    Conclusions. Ways forward

We suggest some embellishments to this layout. On the right hand in another colour — bold red for instance — you might like to place a reminder to yourself of the various visual aids you had planned to use. With all the nerves generated before and during the actual presentation it is very easy to forget what you had actually planned to do!

On the left-hand side it's not a bad idea when you are rehearsing the talk to jot down how long you intend spending on each section and so how long the whole talk will take. Try to do this properly as if it was the real thing. Talk out loud, put on the slides if you have access to the equipment, and in general allow sufficient pauses as there would be in any live presentation. Pencil these timings along the left-hand margin of your notes. They will give you an approximation of the length of your talk. This can be a great help in reducing those two anxieties mentioned earlier: Have I got enough material or, have I got too much? It is a very good discipline after the talk while its reception is still fresh in your mind (and hopefully in your ears — that applause!) to review those timings to see just how much or how little they corresponded to reality!

There will be times when you may need a fuller script, where these short notes will not be enough. Such an occasion may be where you have to give an academic paper, or as mentioned earlier, where the press will be attending and you have to stick more or less to your script. You may also need a fuller script if you are speaking in a second language where unless you are extremely fluent you may well need more vocabulary and grammatical support.

If the script is fuller then do keep in mind the previous advice about layout — don't clutter up our page. Remember to put in some markers when you can pause — paragraph breaks — and do segregate out your visual aids. Here is an example of a fuller script as used by our transport consultant.

Transport in Cities Options for the C21st

Car growth must be controlled.
If car ownership in the UK
    was to equal telephone ownership we'd need to build
    another: 15000 miles of motorway
                  9000 miles of rural roads
                  not to mention another 12000 large car parks.   *OHP 1*

5   The UK has one of the <u>most rapid increases</u> in car
        ownership in the developed world & one of the smallest
        land masses.

    Governments of all persuasions have over the last
        decade been examining ways of tackling this problem.
    The only consensus that has emerged is
        the <u>need to control cars in cities</u>
    In this talk tonight I would like to provide you with a personal

8   view and offer certain suggestions for
           partial solution — notice I say <u>partial</u>.

     Unless we stop being a democracy and simple order
           people not to use cars
           confiscate cars from them
           then any government will only be able create partial solutions.
     In my view it's not enough to simply control cars in cities
           we need an <u>integrated transport policy</u> —
           that Holy Grail
           that governments have been looking for since the
12   1960s — looking for and never finding!   *OHP 2 cartoon*

     First to Singapore. Since the early 1980s the
           Singapore gov't has introduced a number of
           specific schemes to limit the use of cars in the city.

     Let me remind you of the geography of that state   *OHP 3*

Here as you can see the notes are fuller yet the speaker has attempted to keep the lines short, with key points separated from the main body of the text. He has also retained the left margin for timings and the right for visual aids.

You may in your preparation for the talk like to write it out in this fuller way and then distil these notes into the skeletal form we saw earlier.

Visual aids:

Novice and inexperienced presenters often rush on at this stage to think of what visual aids they want to use. They may reach for the powerpoint display or round up 36mm or overhead projector slides. The more experienced presenter thinks through very carefully what the purpose of talk is and how best to illustrate it. He or she may decide that very little or no visuals will be needed — it's more the direct face-to-face approach. On the other hand because of the need to illustrate a process or system then some kind of visual representation may be required. The important point is that these visuals are complementary to the talk and not just bolt on extras. We'll say more about this on page 92 – 93.

Preparing counters to likely objections:

We've mentioned that the attitudes of an audience will range from the positive, through neutral to hostile. In the detailed preparation of the talk our advanced presenter will think through possible counters to any objections. It will seldom, if ever, be possible to counter all the objections; some will be so buried that no amount of detailed pre talk preparation will be enough to unearth them. But if we do try and put ourselves in the position of our audience we should be able to do some 'countering'.

Here are a few more obvious ones.

Objection: *This is all very well but what about me?*
Counter: Particular examples that relate to people like 'me' to help demonstrate
               the immediacy and appropriacy of the talk.
Objection: *This is all very well but you would say that wouldn't you!*
Counter: Be open: Yes I would say that but I also do believe in it. Personal
               enthusiasm and commitment in the talk will certainly help counter this
               kind of objection. You will also have to select your examples and
               illustrate with credible facts.
Objection: *We're just small; what you say only applies to the 'big ones.'*
Counter: Evidence to demonstrate that small organisations like 'yours' have
               actually benefited from the process, system etc. Again, you will need to
               select your examples with care.
Objection: *Well it's fine but much too expensive.*
Counter: Something on the lines of: 'You need to think of the quality you're
               getting here. The more expensive the product the less likely you are to
               need servicing and spare parts. Given the use you'll be making of the
               product these should weight as important factors in your decision.'
Objection: *Well that's OK overseas but it wouldn't do here.*
Counter: Provide examples where the transfer would work, that there might
               have to be some adaptations but the essentials could be transported
               with benefit to 'here'.

You can see the drift: the advanced presenter will be sensitive to these counters and
will realise that the more sophisticated the audience the more the counters themselves
will need to be sophisticated. Simple rebuttals will not suffice with such an audience;
they will only antagonise or bore them.

Coping with nerves
Before we get to the actual delivery of the talk the advanced presenter will know about
how to cope with nerves, notice we use the word cope, it's impossible to completely
master nerves. Even if you are a very experienced presenter there will still be those
moments when you stand waiting to start when you wished you hadn't agreed to the
invitation. Your hands may be shaking a little, a cold sweat begins to break out on the
forehead and your mind goes blank as to what your first point is.

What the more experienced presenter does is to learn to cope with nerves. He or she
knows that some nerves are a 'good thing' in that they stimulate performance, by the
production of adrenaline. The day when you stride up to the podium with no nerves
and zero apprehension is the day when you may come a cropper! So what are the ways
we can cope?

- Be positive about yourself. Avoid apologising for yourself. There's nothing that puts
  an audience off more than someone beginning their talk with the words:

'I've never done this before', or
'I'm not very good at this' or
'I haven't had much time to prepare this'.

Your audience will not be very impressed by such statements. Be positive not apologetic. We don't mean be arrogant and glare defiantly at your audience but you have been invited, you have something to say and you have some material prepared. So don't apologise, and even if you weren't given much notice or you haven't spoken on this before keep that to yourself.

• The audience will want a success. There are very few audiences which look forward with eager anticipation to a failure. Members of any audience have had to get to the place, use up time in being there that they could spend doing something else, are often seated on hard chairs usually without the chance of a decent drink in their hands, so they don't want a flop. They want something useful, something that can assist them in their work and life. By success we don't mean that kind of dramatic speech which rocks the audience back on their feet, stuns them with amazement and provides you with a standing ovation at the end. We mean that the audience have had a structured talk, which has been audible, of interest, relevant to the title and has kept to the time allotted.

• Get to the venue early. You are not likely to be that successful at coping with your nerves if you have to hurry into a hall already full of people and then be watched as you sort out papers, arrange slides, drag OHP or screens into position, have no time to find a glass of water or discover where the toilets are. Avoid such horrors like the plague. Get to the venue at least half an hour before you are due to start. Sort out your papers, check the equipment, find out where the essentials are.

An experienced presenter knows the importance of getting to the venue early and where possible having a good long look at it. If you're on a stage get up there and get the feel of it. This is also the time before the audience is settled to make all those adjustments which will help you be more confident. These could include:

• Opening windows
• Adjusting light levels
• Moving lecterns
• Practising with mics and adjusting amplification levels
• Testing out slide projectors/powerpoint — focusing them
• Adjusting seating etc.
• Making sure you've got a jug of cold water and a clean glass.

Presenters need to feel reassured with their circumstances. Inexperienced presenters are not assertive enough to ask for the environment to be improved, they soldier on unhappy and this sense of unhappiness eats into their confidence.

Delivery

There is a body of research into presentational skills which suggests that we can enhance our ability to a) gain and b) to hold the attention of audiences if we:

- *Use a good deal of eye contact.*

One way of spotting inexperienced presenters is to see how they focus on a small group usually in front of them and usually those giving off positive expressions of interest or encouragement. This focusing has the effect of rather embarrassing those people while at the same time losing contact with others in the audience. Those who started with rather negative feelings towards the speaker will be unlikely to have such feelings ameliorated if they are never looked at, seemingly never included in the occasion. The advanced presenter has mastered the art of moving his or her gaze from face to face long enough to make a very brief contact and also to be able to gain a general impression from the non-verbal leakage — the various expressions that we give off without being aware of it! (See page 12.)

- *Be audible.*

One of the ways in which inexperienced presenters betray their lack of skill is that they fade in volume. They may begin their talk with reasonable audibility but this decreases as they forget to project their voices in accordance with the size of the audience (the more bodies, the more the sound is absorbed) and the acoustics of the room. Good projection should not be a matter of straining but of being aware of where the voice is going and making effective use of breathing to support the voice. It's no wonder that such presenters often do fail to project: they are usually too busy peering at their notes and being worried by what's coming next.

It is very important that you try and breath deeply and get your breathing under some kind of rhythm. Try also to breath from the bottom of the lungs rather than from the throat. If you use too much throat your voice will sound thin and rasping, and you will probably end up with a sore throat.

- *Taking care of your voice.*

If you speak in public and therefore make demands on your voice do consider careful use and maintenance of it. Here is some advice.

– Do keep hydrated
– Drink water before you talk, sip it during the talk and have a good swallow afterwards.
  Avoid coffee and tea (and spirits) before speaking; these tend to dehydrate
– Try to eliminate muscle strain
  Do some neck and shoulder shrugging before you speak
– Wear clothes that are kind
  Avoid tight collars and waist bands/belts

– Aim to get your breathing into a slow rhythm
   Sit quietly before you stand up to speak; think about your breathing, try to get it into a gentle rhythm.
– Sigh in some deep breaths
– Don't rush your opening
   Get into a comfortable, upright stance; avoid shoulder sag.
   Stand balanced on both feet.
   Check ventilation
   Avoid speaking in a stuffy, airless room. Open some windows.
– Put bowls of water under radiators to redress the balance in the air that is dried out by central heating
– Don't smoke
   Avoid atmospheres where others smoke.
– Smoking and passive smoking dry out the throat and larynx and impair the efficient use of lungs.
– Don't push a tired voice. Rest it

• 　　*Making use of microphones.*
If it is at all possible try to use your natural voice without any amplification. Very often with just a little more projection you will be heard. Amplification can reduce the quality of your voice and its tone colour.

However where you need to use a loop system and where the room is large and the audience are many then you will need to use a mic.

Here are some suggestions for you to consider.

Always get into the room/hall early and test out the system in advance.
Speak some words into it and, if possible, have someone who will sit in different areas of the room/hall to give you feedback on audibility.
Ask this person such questions as:
　　　　　Is my voice too loud or soft?
　　　　　Does my voice sound thin?
　　　　　Does my voice sound clear?

If you are not using enough breath support the voice will sound thin.
If you are standing too near the mic the words may sound fuzzy and unclear.
If you are standing too far away then the voice will not be amplified.
If you are sounding the 'p' and 'b' with too much effort the sound will be amplified producing a popping effect.

Always take your time when you start to speak into the microphone. It is important to allow an extra second or so to let the ends of your words resonate around the space. Allow your audience to 'tune in'.

Have confidence to finish a sentence; allow for that to end before anything else is said. It is similar to the silence after the orchestra has sounded the last note of music.

Final point.

Do have a good look at where the speakers are placed; it may be possible by moving these slightly- turning them into your audience- that you will improve the quality of sound.

- *Sound enthusiastic.*

There's nothing like a speaker who has fire in the belly, who appears to believe in the message and is not just spouting out lifeless phrases with little zest or sparkle. As we have seen the inexperienced speaker has so much to worry about, like the learner driver, that enthusiasm is often left behind as he or she struggles to overcome the apprehension and get to grips with the basics. This is a great shame as it gives rise to the audience not being convinced and probably bored. How do we signify to our audience that we are enthusiastic and that we do believe in our message?

As we have seen eye contact is crucial as is the ability to vary the pace and tune of the voice. If we are enthusiastic about something then the tune of voice becomes more varied, there is stress on the words we think are important and there is an intensity in the pace. When we are bored the tune is flat, there isn't that intensity in tone and the pace tends to drag.

- *Start slowly.*

The inexperienced speaker often starts too fast, everything about the opening is rushed. There's a sense of hurry; not only is it difficult to make out what he or she actually says but there's just too much fussing with papers, notes, equipment, adjusting lecterns etc.

A slow start reassures your audience. Remember they have to tune in to you, your voice, your appearance, your subject matter. If you rush these first moments they will not be able to tune in and some will never 'find the place'. Watch advanced speakers and you will probably see them pause for several seconds before they start; they will gather themselves ready, get their breathing under control, look up and out towards the faces in front of them — and then start.

- *Effective opening or point of entry.*

It is important to get a good beginning. Apart from introducing yourself and subject you should think carefully of what point of entry will stimulate your listeners and at the same time form a springboard into the main themes of your talk.

An example of this would be to find a statistic or quote which would stimulate your audience and make it easier for you to launch into your talk. Here's is an opening for a talk to a Rotary Club lunchtime meeting on Exporting: the Challenges and Opportunities.

> I can transport a bottle of Scottish whisky to Japan, unload it at the docks, carry it 500 miles across country, deliver it to a local store, and still sell it for half the price I could buy it at my off-licence round the corner here in Glasgow!

That should get their interest and it also leads into one of the key themes of the presentation — understanding the international market and its strange pricing systems is a must for the would be exporter.

When thinking about your openings keep your audience and their 'needs' very firmly in mind. A good opening can make the talk; a poor, inappropriate, lame one can seriously weaken it. Do be careful of starting with a joke, make sure that it won't cause offence and that it isn't too well known.

• *Provide a structure and keep to time.*
As we listen intently to an advanced presenter we may be aware that the talk is structured, that we are being led from point to point and then into a conclusion and all this is done within a couple of minutes of the allotted time.

Inexperienced presenters will find it difficult to keep to time. On the one hand they have prepared too much material and then have to 'toboggan' to their conclusion, rushing over key points and running the risk of leaving their audience bewildered. On the other hand they have under prepared and have to face one of the most embarrassing of all public speaking experiences — running out after ten minutes with your audience expecting the full half hour.

> Well...I think at this point...I'll...
> Are there, are there...any...questions?
> Questions relating to what I've just said...?
> Anyone...Anything...?

More experienced speakers will be able should this happen to bluff their way through.

> Before I go on to the rest of my talk *(of which there isn't any)* this is a good time to see if there are any questions about what I've just said. Was it clear?

> Did you all agree with my premise...Anyone not?...
> Yes, the gentleman in the front...*(who hasn't actually said anything but has leaked an expression of concern)*

What happens now is that the second part of the talk is made up of answers to the various questions posed and the discussion that the presenter generates. He or she winds up with a summary of the key points that have emerged and comes to a speedy, snappy conclusion. Do keep your eye very firmly on the clock — time can run away very quickly when you make use of this strategy.

We are not suggesting that you should make a habit of this kind of approach but if you do for any reason find yourself running short of material it is a very useful gambit to employ.

- *Using visual aids appropriately.*

We've already said that any visuals should be complementary to the presentation and not bolt-on extras. Make sure that you like using them, that they appeal to you. What is there about the advanced presenter and his or her use of visuals? We could draw up a list:

Visuals used are *clear*. The audience does not have to squint to see them.

The print is *bold*. Inexperienced presenters often make the great mistake of photocopying pages from books and using these as slides — the print is far too small.

These days most presenters make some use of overhead, 36mm slides or increasingly PowerPoint presentations. Here's some advice about each of these.

– OHP and 36mm slides

The important thing here is not to overuse these. You may have experienced the situation where you were presented with a veritable blizzard of slides all packed into a fifteen minute presentation — you had hardly focused on the one when it was whisked away and replaced by another. So,

- Don't overuse — go for quality not quantity. It's better to have 3 or 4 slides of real quality (in terms of information and graphical design) per 15 minute presentation than 10 – 12.
- Don't put too much on the one slide. Avoid as we've mentioned, photocopying pages from a book and making these into slides: the print is almost always too small to be of any use and the diagrams are too often unreadable from the back of the room. It is much better to:
  - Print in large letters and use bold. We suggest 14 – 16 point print size and bold.
  - Leave plenty of space between the lines; use wide margins and something like 6 lines or 6 words per line per slide.
  - Introduce the slide before you show it. If you put on the slide and start talking few of your audience will be listening to you, they will be focusing on the visual — your words will be lost.

In general, you need to design your slides as slides and not as anything that looks like a page.

Do make sure that you test out any visuals before you use them. If you're using 36mm slides do make sure that they are not full of dust and fingerprints. Clean the top of the OHP for any fingerprints or smears.

A word of caution on humorous slides. The cartoon humour that comes from downloading clip art should be avoided. What used to be funny a few years ago has become routine and 'naff' these days. If you want to use humour in slides then hunt around for cartoons and pictures that appeal to you.

– Powerpoint and other computer aided displays

Such displays are particularly suited to showing processes, movement, flows, statistical data which can be changed before your eyes etc. They are less useful for text and too often in our experience the audience can become bored by endless words moving across the screen. Our advice is to use PowerPoint for graphical displays and keep the text very limited. Try to avoid having yourself as presenter blacked out as you speak. There should be some low light on you otherwise all the audience will hear is a disembodied voice. Remember that in some programs it is difficult to go backwards in your presentation so take care as to your structure. Computer systems will let you down one day so have some OHP slides with you as a back up. If the OHP fails then always carry some flip charts pens!

Making Powerpoint work for you — Key tips.
• Reduce your slides to the absolute minimum- don't bore your audience • Never try to compete with your slides. Explain them first and then show them. Remember your audience can't read and listen all at the same time. If you talk and show then they'll stop listening. • Exploit Powerpoint to show graphs and maps- in fact complex information that it is so good at doing. • Do avoid fancy effects. Your audience has probably seen them before. • Avoid clip art- it's all been seen before • To keep the attention of the audience on you for an important part of the presentation- a key message- use blank slides. This will encourage them to focus on your words. • Please don't have a slide which says 'The End' or 'Goodbye'

Building a rapport with your audience

Although we are there to provide information we are also aiming to build a positive relationship with the audience. There will be those who will remain negative to you and your information so you hope by using the various techniques we've listed above to be able to build up a positive relationship with those faces out there.

One of the best ways is to allow the lighter moments to be expressed. Inexperienced presenters see humour as a matter of planned jokes, carefully rehearsed stories and anecdotes and cartoons put on slides. These techniques are not without merit but they have to be planned with care, thinking of the needs and make up of your audience. You have to remember that when you use such planned humour there is always a risk that it won't work, that the humour will die in front of you and there will be that embarrassing pause when you have to pick yourself up and start again. That said there is always a place for the clever, the witty, the unusual joke, anecdote. If it appeals to you, i.e. you enjoy the humour then go for it but don't worry if all your audience don't fall about with mirth!

The 'best' humour is very often that which emerges from the nature of your presentation, of your being up there and in front of that group of people on that occasion. This is the spontaneous kind which can bubble up quite unexpectedly. The important point is that you, as the presenter, have to be aware of the possibility for humour and allow it to escape — this means that you have to enjoy those moments of lightness and smile and chuckle along with the audience. Humour is infectious, use your smiles and chuckles to infect your audience.

If the topic of the presentation is essentially serious then it is important for there to be the lighter moment, this will provide some contrast for the audience; the serious side will appear to even more so if there has been this slight variation in mood.

- *Coming to a conclusion.*

Inexperienced presenters often allow their talks to peter out. A strong conclusion is important because it sets the scene for the question and answer session and it can help to reinforce a few key points in the mind of the audience. One of the oldest pieces of advice about presentation is:

> SAY WHAT YOU'RE GOING TO SAY (your introduction)
> SAY IT (the main body of your talk) and finally
> SAY WHAT YOU'VE SAID (the conclusion).

Recap on the key points. Always leave your audience with a key idea, a central theme for them to take away.

Handling questions

The inexperienced presenter can flounder here. If he or she has not put in sufficient counters to likely objections this is where handling the question session can be a torture: your weakness in argument and factual accuracy can be mercilessly exposed. The question and answer session can however be the best of the presentation: it can enliven proceedings, help build your credibility with your audience and ensure that your key points are hammered home.

If members of your audience ask you questions then it is a fair bet that they have found something of interest, something to challenge or a point that requires further expansion. They may of course just being kind to you because the presentation has fallen a bit flat!

Too many speakers make little or no effort to prepare themselves for questions; this is dangerous. As you prepare your material consider:

> What are likely to be the difficult, contentious points raised?
> Am I going to say anything that might shock or be uncomfortable for my audience to hear?
> Are there any facts I intend using which might raise doubts?

Remember what we stated earlier in this chapter: you will need to prepare counters in your presentation to possible objections. No matter how well you do this there will always be those aspects of your talk which will stimulate questions. So be prepared. Make sure you have double checked those facts!

Managing questioners. Many speakers state at the start of their talks that they are very ready to take questions. Some even say:

'If you want to ask me anything, just stop me as I go along, OK?'

If you do say this then you must mean it. You will need to be very certain of your material and your ability to time yourself to be able to fully accept this rule. Some speakers say this and then look decidedly uneasy when that first question hurtles to them from some inquisitive person eager to take up the invitation!

Do think very carefully if you do actually want to take questions at any time. It's fine if there's no hurry and it's just a small audience but you can get yourself easily side-tracked by taking questions in this way and this can lead to the familiar result of having to 'toboggan' to your finish.

You may now be thinking, but surely offering this 'facility' to your audience is a good thing — it's part of customer care is it not. Well yes, is our answer but better to provide definite breaks in your talk when you can come to the end of a particular section and know that's where you've reached in your plan. The longer and more complex the presentation the more your audience may appreciate the chance of asking you questions at certain intervals rather than having to wait until the end. The other advantage of having questions at set intervals in the talk is that if you leave them until the end many of your audience will have to rush away to feed parking meters, go to their next engagement etc. On the other hand there is a danger that the flow and rhythm of your presentation could be broken if you have various stoppages on the way.

Being your own chair. It is a great advantage to have a chairperson who will take the strain of spotting the questioner, watching the time, balancing the various 'interests and being stern with any troublemakers!

Assuming that you don't have a chair and that you have to be your own here's some practical advice:
- Keep your eye on the time
- Take one question only from any individual. (say you'll take more if there's time)
- Try and balance the sides of the room (i.e. not all from your right or left or straight ahead)
- Try also to balance different categories of your audience such as in a university audience:

  'Are there any questions from students on the courses?' i.e. we've only had questions from staff !

Be sure to announce that there will time for one/two more questions and stick to that limit. If you are prepared to hang about after the presentation, and you should certainly if at all possible do so (see next section).

Answering the question. Here are some strategies for you.
- Answer directly as possible and then check back with the questioner:
  'Is that clear?' or 'Does that answer your point?'

- Answer it in part and then present it to the audience as a question so that other views can be collected. You can then act as chair during this session.

  'Well, that's how we see it, does anyone else have a view on this issue?

You can then supply some further clarification or amplification. Do be careful that you don't get drawn into an elaborate conversation; remember there well may be others wanting to ask questions.

- Say that you can't answer it now, because the question raised is too narrowly focused to be of interest to the rest of the audience and that you'll see that person after the talk.
- Say that you haven't got the information to hand and that you will send it on if they leave their name and address. This is the appropriate tactic when you really haven't got the answer. There is absolutely no point in trying to bluff your way through an answer if in your own mind you are unsure.

These are all tactics that you can use if you have questions but what should you do if at the end of your presentation and the call for questions there is a complete silence? Well you can ask open questions which may serve to trigger off responses, as in:

Can I ask would most of you accept the view I've been advocating on.......?

Or you might refer back to an earlier point made in the talk when you detected that you had stirred some members of the audience into agreement or disagreement, as in:

I noticed in the middle of the talk when I mentioned the problems with...... that some of you appeared to disagree. Would anyone like to raise a question on this?

There's no guarantee that any of these tactics will prove 100% fail-safe but at least they provide you with some chance of stirring up a question. One the most important ways of getting questions after a presentation is to pitch the presentation in such a manner that it so stimulates the audience that as soon as you the speaker have finished they want to get in on the act.

The awkward type. If you do receive a rude, hostile or discourteous question which appears to be an attack on you and those who you represent, then do try and stay calm. The audience will be very much on your side if you can stay calm and not be provoked. It's very tempting to retaliate and bite back. This will play directly into the hands of the questioner. Stay calm, count to 10 and respond on the lines of:

'I think it's best for us to discuss this later'.
'You're fully entitled to your opinion. Can I respond to the general point you've made'....
(i.e. ignoring the personal attack!)

Final point about handling questions. If it is a formal meeting always check before you start your presentation with the chair of the session as to the ground rules for questions and any time limits you need to be aware of.

After the presentation

The inexperienced presenter is so glad to finish that he or she will probably scuttle off the stage and away from the hall, or only stopping briefly to grab a cup of coffee or something stronger!

Our more experienced colleague realises that this time is crucial for developing further contacts with the audience. This is when if you can spare the time individual enquires can be addressed, business cards exchanged, meetings arranged etc. It is very foolish to arrange another engagement straight after a presentation. Many organisers do try and arrange sandwiches, coffee or some kind of snack after such an event and although there will be times when you have to dash off, avoid making this a habit. If you do you will lose out on some very fruitful developments.

As we have said earlier in the section on attitudes there will always some who will never be moved by what you say but there will be a few who might just be persuaded if you can meet them face-to-face. Still others might come a little way to meet you if you could visit or telephone them after the talk, so stay around and collect names and addresses.

Conclusion

We've mapped out some of the differences between the inexperienced and the advanced presenter. Because of the limitations of space this has been a very condensed analysis. Please refer to the suggested follow up reading.

Presentation is a skill and like all the communication skills outlined in this book requires much practice and feedback. One very important form of feedback is that from self-reflection, (as outlined on pages 4 – 5), so try and do some reflection and analysis after you have given your presentation. Treat yourself after the event to something nice, sit down with a cappuccino and a slice of cake, or whatever is your idea of a treat, and just run over what happened and what your feelings were. Have a look at those notes you made for that presentation and while the memories are fresh, jot down a few thoughts as to what, if anything, might have been done differently, what extra visual aids might have been used, what examples could have been introduced. Jot down also what went well and what can be re-inforced if you were to give the presentation again.

Giving a presentation is a challenge; if you do it well it can be a very satisfying experience and one that can enhance your reputation with colleagues, clients and yourself.

Further reading

C. T. Goodworth, *Effective Presentation*, Business Books, 1984

R. Ellis & A. McClintock, *If You Take My Meaning*, Arnold, 1994

The ingredients of effective writing

No one can pretend that writing is easy, for many people it is an extremely difficult business, full of reminders of school exercises and the sheer drudgery of having to get thoughts down on paper clearly, concisely and rapidly.

Before looking in more detail at the actual processes of writing we should at this stage examine the key criteria — the effective ingredients that go to make for successful writing.

It might be useful if you just jot down on a bit of paper what you would put down as your chief criteria. Think of those reports and memos and letters that you have read, or tried hard to read, what made them readable, what could have made them more readable and so what would go into your list?

Here's ours.

Being concise

This is a major ingredient of most writing — that is being able to write what you have to in a reasonably brief manner. By concise we mean avoiding waffle and getting to the key point without flab. Bernard Shaw once replied to a correspondent: 'I'm sending you a long letter because I haven't got time to write you a short one', and there's some truth in this. Most of us can fill a couple of pages with flannel but when asked to distil our thoughts into a single paragraph we will inevitable struggle since every word has to carry meaning.

Although being concise is a vital ingredient we need to be able to balance it with the need to be comprehensive. There's little point in being concise if vital elements, key facts, key costings etc. are left out. There's another issue and that is that certain readers make a correlation between the number of pages produced and the perceived merit of the text. So if you hand your reader a couple of paragraphs as the fruits of your labour he or she may very well glance through it having 'weighed' it in the hand, and adjudge it accordingly. Making judgements according to the weight of documents is understandable given the fact that in the academic world one requires some 50,000 words for a bachelor's degree, 80,000 for a Master's and over 100,000 for a PhD, hence a connotation that weight equals rigour. We can see this in the following phrases:

- A good thick book
- A weighty tome
- A substantial text
- A good long read.

All these phrases denote the positive value that is attributed to heavy texts whereas the words associated with conciseness — slim report, short text, brief note, etc. these often imply a lack of depth, of rigour and of serious application.

We as writers and readers have to resist this negative impression and praise those who provide us with crisp documents. This is why we should produce summaries for our 'customers' so as to give for them the essential information. Most people don't want to be submerged with detail, they want the key facts and figures. We should help them in this at the same time we should resist the demands for everything to be put into bullet points; some complex issues cannot be reduced to this extent: it can lead to dangerous simplification.

Over the years the author has carried out a number of communication audits; often one of the stumbling blocks to flows of communication in organisations is the sheer amount of paper (increasingly electronic text based) that flows around. What is needed is for summaries to be made of key texts and for these summaries to be circulated. For those really who do need to have the full text there should be provision for such to be sent. Such a system might avoid the practice of mass photocopying and mass distribution of substantial texts that often end up in cupboards unread and unmarked. Large organisations might consider appointing specialists such as retired journalists who could perform this abstracting service. Obviously this person would need to be familiar with the material and the needs of the audience.

Being clear

Writing is a constant struggle for clarity unless we think of poetry which is often constructed so that it can remain ambiguous and open to various meanings. In the writing we are concerned with in this book we are seeking to carry meaning from us to our reader, who will create meaning from the words we write. We have to remember that clarity is in the eye and ear of the reader. We may feel confident that what we have written is clear and unambiguous but the crucial test is can our reader understand it, can our reader make sense of it? One way to check on this is to show a draft to others, if possible those who are as similar as possible to your actual readers. This will never provide a perfect test because your test reader cannot fully simulate the reactions of your target reader; he or she may say that the text is clear in order to spare your feelings, or may just not be bothered enough to give it a serious read. We will refer you to page 111 the quote from Earnest Gowers: 'Put yourself in your reader's position....' and that is perhaps the best advice we can give; try and stand back from your writing, hold it at arm's length and ask yourself: 'Will my reader understand this?' Am I making assumptions which are unjustified?

When we think of ambiguity we tend to think of the more obvious kinds such as:

Dogs, please shut all gates before you leave
Remove all clothes before giving this doll to a child under 3.
I have been driving for over 30 years. I must have fallen asleep when it happened.

The ambiguity in these examples is fairly obvious and unlikely to go unrecognised, in fact a good deal of humour is generated by such ambiguities. The really dangerous forms of ambiguity are those where after a first, even second reading all seems clear and there appears to be no ambiguity. Here, for example, is an extract from a manual on the installation of a complex radar system. What would you understand this to mean?

> The panels used in this system contain several circuit components; they have been specifically designed to withstand very low temperatures, i.e. those in excess of -30C.

Is that clear? Are there ambiguities? Is it for instance obvious what the word 'they' refers to? Is it panels or components? We might suggest that it is more likely to be components because that noun is closer to the 'they' than the word panels but it is not certain and therefore an element of doubt is created. Would you be entirely happy with the final phrase,' in excess of -30C'. Does the word 'excess' create a difficulty when placed next to a negative amount? Do two negatives then make a positive? These doubts could prove troublesome for the reader who has to make precise judgements and calculations, who may have to give up extra reading time and effort in order to clarify what is unclear and deduce what may be hidden. It is just not possible, except in isolated cases, to phone, fax, e-mail the writer and ask for clarification; this kind of concealed ambiguity creeps through undetected and can have serious and often expensive consequences.

Here is another example, an extract from a building society's letter to customers who intend taking out personal loans.

> *Loan Agreement*
> Please sign and insert the date of your signatures in the box provided on the Agreement marked SIGNATURE COPY in the top left corner.

This at first reading may appear clear but the author found it ambiguous and so did several of his friends and work colleagues he showed it to. How would you re-write it so as to make it easier to read? Is there for instance some indication that the signatures should go in the top left corner? Is this how you read it? What might have helped would have been to divide the sentence into two separate ones and make it clear what each was about, as in:

> Please find the agreement marked SIGNATURE COPY, this will be found in a box at the top left corner of page 3.
> Would both of you please sign and insert the date in the appropriate places at the bottom of this page.

Do you find this easier to read? It separates the place (the special paper) from the action (the signature and the dating); these were placed together in the same sentence.

It is to sentences that we now turn for the next ingredient.

Being Readable

These days of word processors, each with a sophisticated software program for spell and grammar checking, it is surely possible, one might think, to find a method of testing written material so that is readable. This is not the place to go into detail on readability measurements but briefly most software programs make use of the work of two researchers, Flesch and Gunning. They made use of two variables: the average length of sentences in a given sample and the number of syllables in a 100 words. Gunning examines the number of polysyllabic words (of more than two syllables) while Flesch counts the number of syllables. Gunning is careful to suggest that the sample of text for readability measurement should not to be taken from the opening section because, he notes, writers are on their best behaviour and are conscious of the need to be readable, whereas once they get into their stride they revert to their bad old habits!

When you access a readability score on your word processor — you will normally find these under the grammar check option — you will receive a numerical score; the higher the number the better the readability, so, for instance, Ladybird books will be up in the 90s since their sentences are not normally more that 10 words in length and they use plenty of short words. Compare that to a text book on physics which may have many sentences of 25 words, each full of polysyllabic words. In this case the score on the readability index could be 35 – 40 which comes out as a very unreadable text .

There are various difficulties with such measurements. Firstly, there is sufficient research into readability to suggest that some longer sentences are in fact easier to read than some shorter ones; secondly, that there are many short words of one or two syllables which are easier to read than longer words. Stasis (sta I sis) a two syllable word is more difficult to read for most people than governmentally, (gov I ern I ment I al I ly) a five syllable one. Thirdly, when making use of such readability measures we need to remember that they are using only two variables, whereas we shall be listing many more than that in this chapter.

For instance, we may be scoring well in terms of readability, shortish sentences and not too many long words, but is the text clear and free of ambiguity? There's also the point that short sentences in themselves may be useful but if that is all that we write we may not only appear to patronise our reader but also bore them. Have you ever tried to read a text full of short sentences? Many people have got hold of the Plain English message, one that states that long sentences are not good, which is sensible advice but there's no need to reduce all your writing to short staccato sentences. What is needed is variety of length, some longer sentences, some shorter. There is no doubting the difficulties posed for readers when they are presented with a whole string of long sentences (i.e. those of 25 words and over).

We can introduce variety in our writing if we use a range of sentences. Writing a shortish sentence amidst longer ones can create emphasis for that shorter sentence, as in this example:

The introduction of this new readability checker will provide writers with a valuable tool.

103

It is the first such aid on the market. It will assist all those who have to write for a wide
audience since, with the detailed advice available in this program and the many examples
provided, writers will be more able to pitch their material so that it will be more readable.

Notice how the second sentence, much shorter than the others, underlines a key selling
point. The third sentence is quite long and certainly could be broken into two but that
might run the risk of making the whole text too jerky and broken up.

The moral here is do not put too much faith in readability measures. Keep a
watchful eye on longish sentences. For instance is this readable?

Too many people are dependent on spell checkers to verify their documents when using
this function on their PCs, since research points to the fact that it is wise to give all texts a
thorough read through, an old-fashioned proof reading, that is taking nothing for granted
and subjecting each word, each comma, each phrase etc., to the closest possible scrutiny.

If you think this is readable then you must have a good digestion, for most readers
there are just too many separate bits of information to be 'swallowed' in one chunk.

*Before reading on you might like to consider how you would re write this sentence so as
to make it more readable, for instance how many separate sentences you would create
out of this specimen.*

Here is our suggestion:

Too many people are dependent on spell checkers to verify their documents. When using
this function on the PC it is wise, according to research, to give all texts a thorough read
through. This old-fashioned proof reading means taking nothing for granted and
subjecting each phrase, word and comma to the closest possible scrutiny.

Here we have changed the long sentence into several shorter ones. We have tried to
observe a key principle that every sentence should have one main idea in it and not the
3 or 4 apparent in the original version. At the same time we have tried not to make the
text too staccato and broken up.

Finding the right tone

There is a sense that what we write is what we mean, i.e. because we have committed
to paper these thoughts then they must have been meant and intended. We compare
this to speech which many feel is a more ephemeral media, it's off the cuff, 'Well it just
came out and wasn't deliberately meant', we may say. We know that it is not really
possible to make such a distinction. Some spoken 'texts' are as deliberately constructed
as any written ones and we know that many e-mails are just rapidly thrown together
without much in the way of preparation. However, the popular notion is that written
texts — even e-mails — are deliberate and this means that we have to be very careful

as to the tone we adopt. Here for instance is the opening of a letter to a candidate who has been rejected after interview:

> It is very much regretted that you have not been selected for the above post. The company wish you good fortune in your search.

This we think you'll agree is cold and impersonal. The use of the passive structure: (see page 123 for details on active and passive) 'It is regretted', is not appropriate for such a letter and more suited to objective reports and requests for payment. The use of the impersonal 'The company' also gives it a remote distant feeling. How would you have phrased such a letter? How about:

> We are sorry to inform you that you have not been selected for the above post. Thank you for your interest; we wish you all the best for future applications and for your future.

You may feel that this is laying it on a bit much and that no matter how pleasant the letter, the nature of the disappointing news means that any such text is unlikely to more than glanced at. However civility costs nothing!

There are certain words and phrases which can trigger off reader resentment as to the tone adopted. We've already looked at transactional analysis which depicts how, if we use a 'Parental' tone, we may well trigger off a 'Childish' response. This explains why we need to be careful when sending off e-mails when we are in a bad mood. By so doing we can trigger off many angry children in the organisation; remember we have to live with them afterwards. It is good advice to sleep on a letter which was written in anger and look at it in the cold light of day; we may well then decide not to send it. With e-mails being sent at the touch of a button there is much less chance that these will be 'slept on' and much more likely that they will be sent hot down the line to smoulder on a colleague's or client's PC. Here is an extract from a memo that was e-mailed throughout an organisation. What do think about the tone?

Dress at work

> On my last tour of inspection round the plant I was surprised, to put it mildly, how many of you were rather slovenly in your turn out. Every member of the staff should be wearing smart uniform, that is clean and pressed. We do have agreed company guidelines on this matter. Read them! Ladies — white blouses, blue/black skirts or trouser suits. Men dark jacket and trousers or suit, company tie, white, grey or blue shirts only!
>
> Remember the impression of smartness and efficiency that we give to our customers is vital. Please act. NOW. I expect to see a marked improvement during my next tour.
>
> Managing Director

Would you like to underline what you consider to be the triggers in this memo, i.e.

those words which are 'parental' and are likely to trigger off a 'childish' reaction in the readers. You might have selected: 'inspection'; 'slovenly'; 'NOW'; 'I expect' as having a parental tone to them. You might like to try your hand at re-writing this memo, trying to keep it in the adult.

Here is our version:

Dress at Work

> Could I take this opportunity to remind all staff as to the importance of keeping to agreed company guidelines on dress at work. The impression of smartness that we give to our customers is vital.
>
> These guidelines were drawn up last year after discussion between management and staff association. They can be found in full on staff workroom notice boards. In summary they state:
>
> Men to wear a dark jacket and trousers or suit; company tie and white, grey, blue shirt. Ladies white blouse, blue/black skirt or trouser suit.
>
> Your co-operation please.

Notice in this second version the reason for the dress code is placed first, not the inspection or the phrase 'I have been extremely surprised' Although it is much more adult the strength of the message is still the same: please act on these guidelines. We can be assertive and still behave as adults. We are not saying that one cannot be frank in one's opinions it's just that we should avoid being personal, wounding and parental in tone, we've already seen the importance of this in our section on listening and interviewing. As e-mails become so much part of our working lives so we need to be alert to the effect of *how* we communicate as well as that from the information we transmit.

Being Consistent

This ingredient is particularly important when one is engaged in a lengthy document; readers will become irritated and even alarmed if you fail to show consistency in your approach to such things as spelling, punctuation an grammar, as in:
- 1990's or 1990s?
- Driving license (US) or driving licence (British)
- Active: I interviewed all the staff, or
- Passive: All staff were interviewed
- E mail or e-mail or email?

You as writer may be provided with guidance as to 'house style', which means the way things are done in your organisation. Often there will be no guide and you will need to seek advice. The important thing is to be consistent; try to avoid having different forms throughout your text; make use of the search and replace facility on your word processor to ensure that there is a consistency.

Being relevant

We will see in the next section that we have to ask and have answered key questions about what it is we are supposed to write. Such questions help us to explore and clarify our remit. This then provides us with a map of what it is we are supposed to do. The danger, having asked these questions and established this map, is that we get stuck into the task and being so absorbed forget what it is we've 'promised' to do. We then move out of the map and into our own 'country'. This is where so many writers (and speakers) fall down: they become increasingly irrelevant. They go on long asides and by ways and forget what it is they're supposed to be actually writing about. This explains why so many promising exam essays do not gain good grades — they have wandered off the topic that was set and moved into the topic that they want to write about; dangerous; very dangerous!

So the message here is check your title/topic/remit and stick with it. Take a few backward glances as you bend over the word processor and check that you're still on target and not wandering off. Asides and rambles can be very pleasant but they can easily loose your reader (and you!).

Finding a suitable structure

We've mentioned maps and maps provide routes. Your reader should be able to see the structure — the backbone — to your text; he or she should not get lost as they read. We will be examining this aspect in more detail when we look at report writing, see pages 128 – 38.

Readers like to know where the text is going, they do not like to become confused. A confused reader can become an annoyed reader and then one who stops reading. You aim as a writer is to 'seduce' your reader into reading through your text from start to final full stop. You therefore need to supply a structure which is easily recognisable. However no matter how good your seduction techniques there are some readers who will drift, skim and scan. This is why the use of headings and subheadings can be so useful to your readers. Think of your main title as a motorway sign — big and bold, say 14 point upper case, then your B headings — the first tier of headings — the A roads, 12 point bold lower case. You might then wish to subdivide your text still further with C headings, the B roads, 12 point and underlined. In this way the reader is provided with clear typographical cues as to the structure of the text — from major to minor.

Apart from supply headings for our readers we also need to think carefully about how we structure the data, the facts, the essentials of our text. We have a number of options.

Here are some possibilities. Remember they can be very useful not only for written texts but also for oral presentations (see pages 91 – 92).

- *Generic*

All the material of the same kind is placed together. This is the most common form of structure, like with like. Inevitably there will come a time when the categories don't quite fit so neatly. If there is a great deal of this overlap, so much so that we fear it will distract our reader, then we may well consider another form of structure.

- *Sequential*

A sequence dictated by the system in operation, the requirements of the client etc.

This is where a flow chart pattern can be very helpful to our readers so that they can follow the pathways as it were.

- *Chronological*

Here we place the text into some form of time structure. It may not appear as smooth as this:

      1960s..........70s..........80s..........90s..........2000

- *Very important to less important: a priority sequence*

Remember simply putting a (1) in the margin may create ambiguity for your reader: he or she may think that this is First and therefore you are creating a priority sequence.

      VIP—————>>>>LIP

We can also move from less important to very important.

- *Spatial*

Here you lay our your material in some spatial, zonal, geographical arrangements which you will make clear to your reader, as in macro spatial:

      North.....east....west....south

or micro spatial:

    the material in this cell as opposed to that one and that,

- *Comparative*

Here we compare one set of information with another as in:

    UK systems of social work training vs Holland's

- *Pros and Cons*

    The fors and against are laid out for your reader:

- *Familiar to unfamiliar*

These structures can be used in combination, i.e. VIP....> LIP with a generic structure running alongside.

Apart from these forms of structuring there are these:

The deductive

You proceed from the general statement (idea or thesis, which we've italicised) to the particulars and illustrations. E.g.:

> *Sugar is particularly harmful to one's teeth.* It attacks the enamel and appears to encourage the formation of plaque; this is turn causes further bacteria to attack the teeth. Many detailed tests have been conducted (British Dental Association 1996) where it has been conclusively shown that those children who have less sugar in their diets have less dental caries and stronger, healthier teeth. Furthermore, in those countries, particular in parts of the Third World, where there is very little intake of sugar, dental caries is almost unknown. True there are many specific disorders of the gums and much in the way of broken and ill formed teeth, but the lack of sugar together with much chewing of meat, vegetables and nuts makes the general dental condition far superior to that found in more affluent countries where the intake of sugar in sweets and cakes is on the increase.

The inductive

Here you proceed from particular details, examples etc. to a general statement (idea or thesis) which serves as a conclusion.

> In those countries, particularly in the Third World, where as yet there is very little intake of sugar, dental caries is almost unknown. True there are many specific disorders of the gums and much in the way of broken and ill formed teeth. But the lack of sugar, together with much chewing of meat, vegetables and nuts makes the general dental condition far superior to that found in countries of the affluent North and West, where the consumption of sugar in the form of sweets and cakes in increasing year by year. Many detailed tests have been conducted on children's teeth (British Dental Association 1996) and these have shown conclusively that those children who have less sugar in their diet have less caries and stronger, healthier teeth. *From this evidence we can safely assume that sugar in diet is the principal cause of rotten teeth.*

As we have noted we will be examining structure again when we look at report writing in the next section.

Appropriate use of graphics

Firstly we should define what we mean here by graphical communication. We refer to the use of tables, pictures, diagrams, maps, histograms, pie charts, x & y graphs, flow diagrams, Gantt charts etc. in fact every possible visual approach to the conveying of information. We are looking at the use of visuals in written texts such as reports and manuals.

You've probably heard the expression, ' A picture is worth 10000 words'. There is a great deal of truth in this but the trouble is that it has become rather a meaningless phrase. It implies that there is some extra special worth in visuals as against mere words. We are sure that you have seen various forms of graphical representation being used which only serve to add 'interest' to an otherwise dull text. There is a mindset at work which says that if you don't pepper your reports with visuals then some of the readers will think that you've rather let them down. However as many of you will know there is always the risk of swamping your reader or listener with unnecessary graphics.

Graphics can be extremely useful and at times absolutely essential. Can you imagine explaining company accounts without use of tables and charts, or progress reports on engineering/science projects without flow charts and graphs. However, this acknowledgement of the desirable nature of graphics should not hide the fact that they can be easily misused, sometimes intentionally but more often than not through ignorance or carelessness.

Some general hints
It always pays to ask yourself the following questions:

Why am I using this graphic?
Do I understood the graphic and the information it contains?
Will my audience understand the graphic?

To help you answer these questions, it is often a good idea before you get into elaborate work on your computer to do some experimenting with pencil and paper. Try out various possibilities. certainly do a trial run of your graphics if possible with a few of the audience that will be reading the graphics. This might give you some useful feedback.

Your audience may not find the graphics as easy to understand as you do. This may be for some of these reasons:

A number of people just do not want to see any graphics. They build up a mental wall against tables or graphs ('I'll never understand this approach' they say, "It's too mathematical and looks difficult'.)

However, for most of the time you will be communicating with people who have had some kind of technical, scientific or technical education. But there will be times when you will wish to communicate to a wider audience so you might want to minimise the technical or mathematical aspects. Secondly, make sure that the pathways are clear, i.e. it is obvious what is the sequence, which 'bits' relate to which. Pay particular attention to x and y axes in the graphs and the way that certain assumptions to do with scale are made explicit.

Take a step back particularly if you do make use of graphics in your writing, and

ask yourself these questions about their use. What are some of the *advantages* of using graphics to communicate? Think carefully before you read our list.
- They can simplify very complex events e.g., power surges
- They can show trends more easily that words, i.e. rises/falls in productivity
- They can dramatise particular effects — sudden shifts for instance
- They can complement the written work — so that we have a written explanation of failures in an operating system which is then followed by a graph highlighting these.

Consider reports etc. that you have read and the graphics that they contained. What have been some of the disadvantages for you the reader?
- Graphics may distort the picture. For instance just showing the last few years' trend on our graphic may distort the real picture
- Graphics may actually lie: the factual basis may be inaccurate
- Graphics will not make poorly written ambiguous text easier to read
- Graphics may overwhelm the written word.

Some principles in the use of graphics
We cannot lay down any precise rules for the use of graphics; much will depend on the house style of the organisation you are working in (for discussion on house style see pages 123). Here is some guidance for you.
- Graphics need to be planned for in any written text rather than simply plonked in. (See section on story boarding on page 124)
- Graphics will not rescue poorly written texts.
- It is vital to quote the sources of your material and the date. Your credibility may well be determined by the acceptability of the sources you quote.
- Think carefully of the nature of the scale of the graphics. You don't want to overwhelm the text with your graphics.
- Be bold. If you are using colour then avoid purples, light blues and yellows. It is highly likely, even with the cost of colour copying becoming more reasonable, that any copy will be in black and white and if you use these faint colours then much of your handiwork will disappear. Be bold also in lettering and design.

Placing the graphics in your report
There are a number of ways in which a graphic can be inserted into a text. Here for instance are some to consider:
1) Placing the graphic in a corner/margin of the text and in small scale but putting the detail, or an expanded version of the graphic, in an appendix at the end of the document, as in:

2) Writing a text on the left-hand page and using the right for graphics.

Text		Graphic

3) Removing all graphics from the text and putting them into an appendix.

4) Placing text and graphic in a complementary position, so that the text enables the reader to understand the graphic and the graphic enables the reader to have a better understanding of the text. This would be our recommended method.

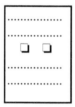

Finding the appropriate register

By this we mean finding the right approach in terms of formality or informality. We will address this issue in letter writing, see pages 138 – 144. Selection of the appropriate register depends very much on the relationships between sender and receiver. We can go from the cold and formal, Dear Sir or Madam to the less formal, Dear Mr/Mrs Smith to the more friendly, Dear John/Susan, then to the more intimate. Jack Darling. Susan Sweetie! or whatever takes your fancy (and theirs!).

In general, it is always better to start a little more formally and then you can ease your way into the less formal. It is very difficult to go the other way round.

Register is very much dependent on the culture in which one is writing. We have already said in our section on presentation that in many countries, India, Japan and much of the Far East, for instance, it is appropriate that you start with the formal. We would certainly recommend that if you are writing to someone from one of these countries, particularly if he/she is someone in a similar profession then you should start with their title, Dear Dr, Dear Professor, Dear Mr and only after you have developed some kind of professional relationship should you become more 'intimate'. There is throughout the world a tendency for younger people to make use of less formal styles in their writing — the advent of e-mail will have contributed to this since it is difficult to sound formal on a screen for some reason. Many older people can be somewhat disturbed when they are greeted by a casual style of writing in letters and requests from those they have never heard of before. We all need to be that little more sensitive to the perceptions and expectations of others. We saw on page 40 the importance of this when telephoning.

Finding the right language

Language should be a bridge between people but sometimes it can be a barrier. We've already noted in various places in this book the importance of tuning in to the others' vocabulary and of thinking carefully about others' language needs. It is no use writing discrete (separate in statistical terms) if our readers are only going to know discreet (keep it to your self). We should to follow those excellent words of Mr Gowers: 'Put ourselves in our readers' shoes'.

There is nothing wrong with using jargon if we have a reasonable idea that those reading our text will also share the jargon. Without jargon it should be so much more difficult for doctors to write to doctors, pilots to speak to pilots and vets speak to vets (never mind their animals!).

It is when we move outside our professional writing zones that we have to be that much more careful to gloss (to explain) our terms. ABM standards might make sense to a US consumer standards officer (American Business Measurements) but to us it might mean Bloody Awful Machines! So do gloss and put all your glosses into your glossary.

Making sure we're accurate in our writing

It almost goes without saying that in all our writing we have to check most carefully for accuracy. We will look at proof reading on pages 126 – 127 but there's also that need to check dates, numbers, prices, names, titles, order numbers etc.

Getting the Nuts and Bolts right

By this ingredient we refer to spelling, punctuation and aspects of grammar. This is such a large area that we could easily take up the remainder of this book with details on each aspect. Here are some key points for revision. Apologies if this is familiar to you.

Spelling

We have already examined some of the problems associated with grammar checkers when we looked at readability on pages 101 – 102. Spell checkers raise similar problems: they recognise words which are in their dictionary. The question is what kind of dictionary do you have. You may posses a Webster's based dictionary; this means that you will have US English spellings as in the previous example license for license and defense for defence. Even if you have a dictionary based on British English your spell checker will face a real challenge when it comes to homophones — those words with similar sounds but very different meanings, e.g. practise, practice; stationery and stationary.

There is some evidence that the advent of the Web with its predominant US spelling is influencing users to spell program as programme, center for centre and donut for doughnut. Here is a little exercise to test your powers to distinguish between homophones. The answers are on page 113 – 114.

1. Shall we accept/except her invitation?
2. His words effected/affected me greatly
3. He decided after punishment to amend/emend his ways
4. Can you insure/ensure/assure me that the brakes are OK?
5. That's a classical/classic example of his behaviour.
6. She was very complimentary/complementary about his new suit.
8. Could you please test the current/currant on this wire?
9. I council/counsel you to accept his advice/advise
10. China's economical/economic growth has been spectacular
11. He immigrated/emigrated into the UK
12. This lock will insure/ensure your safety.
13. He saw a flair/flare of light in the distance
14. It was a historical/historic first journey to Mars
15. The book had lost its/it's cover
16. The boats moored at the key/quay
17. Lightening/lightning his burden he continued up the mountain
18. I license/licence you to sell drugs
19. She was the principle/principal conductor for the orchestra
20. The prophecy/prophesy will come true
21. He practices/practises his golf swing in the garden
22. He was a sceptic/septic as far as religion was concerned
23. The truck was stationery/stationary when we hit it
24. They/their/There book is their/there/they're on the table
25. Two/too/to people watched the film but it was too/two/to long.
26. The waste/waist left after the meal was appalling
27. Your/You're the only person who can succeed.
28. Its/It's you're/your turn now.
29. As a referee you must be uninterested/disinterested in the final result.
30. The police search was exhausting/exhaustive.

Punctuation

Punctuation is a very complex matter; there are certain rules and there are many instances where you can make a judgement. The important advice here is be consistent.

We've set you a little test. Take a piece of paper and a pencil and see how you get on. If this test shows gaps then revise carefully would be our advice.

Each of the following sentences requires some punctuation, put in the commas, full stops etc. that you think should be included.
1. The customers letter included a cheque for £5000 don't cash it
2. Although we installed the new laser printer fuses are still blowing.
3. Mr Fred Jones the general manager of Jones Electronics gave a talk on safety.
4. Remember to check the following
   • ice axe

- climbing boots
- gaiters
- rope

_____

Answers to spelling test — homophones

1. Shall we accept her invitation?
2. His words affected me greatly
3. He decided after punishment to amend his ways
4. Can you assure me that the brakes are OK?
5. That's a classic example of his behaviour.
6. She was very complimentary about his new suit.
8. Could you please test the current on this wire?
9. I counsel you to accept his advice/advise
10. China's economic growth has been spectacular
11. He immigrated into the UK
12. This lock will ensure your safety.
13. He saw a flare of light in the distance
14. It was an historic first journey to Mars
15. The book had lost its cover
16. The boats moored at the quay
17. Lightening his burden he continued up the mountain
18. I license you to sell drugs
19. She was the principal conductor for the orchestra
20. The prophecy will come true
21. He practises his golf swing in the garden
22. He was a sceptic as far as religion was concerned
23. The truck was stationary when we hit it
24. Their book is there on the table
25. Two people watched the film but it was too long.
26. The waste left after the meal was appalling
27. You're the only person who can succeed.
28. It's your turn now.
29. As a referee you must be disinterested in the final result.
30. The police search was exhaustive.

Answers to punctuation test

Question 1

The customer's (1) letter included a cheque for £5000 but don't (2) cash it (3)

(1) We need an apostrophe 's . These show who or what owns something, e.g.

the worker's tools
the dentist's drill
the footballer's boots etc.

When there is more than one person who owns something, the apostrophe comes **after the s**, e.g.
workers' tools (i.e. many workers)
dentists' drills
footballers' boots

With people, children, men, women the apostrophe always comes **before** the s, e.g.
people's safety
children's shoes,
women's clothes

With peop**le's** names which end in an s, such as the autho**r's** Ellis, you can either write
Ellis's books
Ellis' books
but be consistent.

There is no need to use apostrophes when writing short forms, e.g.
NVQs not NVQ's. VDUs not VDU's

Never use an apostrophe for plurals of words. E.g.
Craft trades not craft trade's
pensionable occupations not pensionable occupation's
All paints at half price, not all paints'(or paint's) at half price

(2) We do need apostrophes, as in the question when we leave out a letter. e.g.
don't for do not
can't for cannot
we're for we are
couldn't for could not
shouldn't for should not etc.
The accountant's coming today for the accountant is coming today

(3) Full stops. These are needed for the ends of sentences. They should be followed by a capital letter.
There is no need to put full stops after initials
R.J. Bolton write as R J Bolton
B. B. C. write as BBC
Be very careful when writing down e-mail addresses that you only put the full stops (dots) in the right place, e.g.

jm smith @ records.flash.net
If you place the dots in the wrong position the message won't get sent and don't
put spaces after the dots!
Never put a dot at the end of the address.

Question 2

Although we installed the new laser printer (1) fuses are still blowing.

(1) We need a comma here after an 'although' expression. The same would be true after
the following:
Therefore, we have to buy more tools
However, she did pass the exam
Lastly, he pulled the plug.

Other uses of the comma include:
Providing emphasis in what you write. You can do this by <u>underlining</u> or if using a
word processor use **bold**. However, a more polite way is to use commas: e.g.

Please apply, before Thursday, if interested in this post.

Compare this to

Please apply before Thursday if interested in this post.

By putting commas round 'before Thursday' we are reminding the reader to hurry
up. Compare these two statements.

Please deliver outstanding money in cash before end of the month.
Please deliver outstanding money, in cash, before end of the month.

The second version has more of punch don't you think? It implies, don't send a
cheque or bring along your credit card — just bring the money!
We also use a comma after

Dear Mr Smith,

In a handwritten letter. There is no need to use it when word processing a letter.
• Use it after a so expression, for instance

There were few CDs in the shop, so she went into town to buy her present.

- Asking questions when writing in an informal style. E.g.

This is the right program, isn't it.

- Separate out descriptions. E.g.

The wall was long, badly maintained and in danger of collapsing. (I.e. it was very close to being a complete disaster)

Normally you do not need to place a comma before the final and in a list like this. However, if you really want to emphasise the *and* then you can.

The wall was long, badly pointed, and in danger of collapsing.

- To separate out parts of dates, addresses etc.

Wednesday July 14th, 1999 is a public holiday in France
He lives at 145 High Street, Elborough, Cheshire.
- To separate out sets of figures. E.g.

In 1998, 30 new houses were built.

- To separate out parts of numbers. E.g.

1,456 1,350,000 (most printed texts do not use this)

- To separate out identical repeated words. E.g.

Whatever is, is right.
Try and tap in, in the hole.

Question 3

Mr Fred Jones, the general manager (1) of Jones Electronics, gave a talk on safety.

1) Capitals. We need capital letters for General Manager as this is a title.
   We need capital letters for
   - Beginning a sentence
   - People's names.

Smith, Jim, Susan

- Places

 Birmingham, Essex, New York

- Titles

Mr. Miss. Head Teacher. Dr. Senior Architect. Chief Planner

- Copyright trade names

Coca Cola

- Short forms BBC. TUC. FA.

Again, our advice is: be consistent in your use of capitals.

Question 4

Remember to check the following (1)
 Ice axe
 Climbing boots
 Gaiters
 Rope
(1) After the words following when you introduce a list then use a <u>colon:</u> the two dots. When you write a list then start each item with a capital letter. E.g.

 Ice axe
 Climbing boots etc.

There's no need to put in full stops at the end of each line in a list, only at the final one.

Other aspects of punctuation

The semi colon ;
 This is used where you have two parts to a sentence and you do not wish to break them with a full stop. The sense is continued across them, as in

 Jim was late today; his car broke down.

Now you could put a full stop after today as in

 Jim was late today. His car broke down.

but you might wish to use a semi colon to continue the sense across — his lateness is after all a consequence of his car breaking down. You could not use a comma as there is no conjunction — joining words which link these two such as and, but, however, if etc.

The question mark
This is used at the end of a statement put as a question.

> Did the architect see the plans?

The exclamation mark
This is used to indicate strong feeling, or humour e.g.

> I'd like that money — how about a Christmas present!
> Come back to me when you've won the lottery!

The dash
These are used in informal writing, short notes, e-mails and friendly handwritten letters. E.g.

> I hope this reaches you on time — if not give me a phone.
> The architect's coming on Tuesday 11 am — could you be here then?

They can be used in more formal writing to indicate a change of thought.

> Looking at the philosophy of love — and that's just not on Valentines' day — we need to keep our emotions separate from our thoughts.

The hyphen (a dash between parts of words)
There are some words that *always need to be hyphenated* as *re-cover* (your sofa) compared with *recover* (getting better from illness).
You should also use a hyphen with such expression as off-putting, in-situ (in place)

There are hundreds of words where you can use hyphens if you want. E.g.

> co-operation and co-contractors (it prevents the double oo)
> mis-spelling (preventing the double ss)
> sub-contractor compared with sub contractor

There is also a need for a hyphen where the specialised meaning of a word, e.g

> In the space below draw a view of a *hop-up*. Compare this with,
> Just *hop up* on the lorry and get some bananas.

This has been a rapid tour round nuts and bolts and the main ingredients of writing. We now examine the process of writing.

Follow-up Reading

K. Judd, *Copy Editing: A practical guide*, Robert Hale, 1995.

The process of writing

Writing, for many people, is the most difficult part of communication. They often have bad memories of their English teachers, of seeing their written work covered in red ink with the ominous words "See Me' written underneath. At work, their confidence may not be helped when managers peer over their shoulders at their screens and check the quality of work on them. Very few of us can write well under such scrutiny.

There is also the fact that writing is a very public matter, one's handiwork is exposed to others' view and this can lead to embarrassment. If you've ever made a spelling mistake in a letter or document and that has been passed round your colleagues for comment you will no doubt remember the awkwardness that followed.

A number of people have a lack of confidence in their writing caused by these and other negative experiences, others are more confident but still find there are gaps which can let them down when it comes to the more formal side of writing. This chapter is designed for both categories and if you are a confident writer then we hope that the advice provided and the various techniques illustrated will help you to be even better.

At this point we should clarify the term 'writing'. For many people these days writing apart from the shopping list and signature on agreements, has been replaced by the word processor. We still use the term writing when we should perhaps be using texting, anyway writing will be the term used in this book to cover everything from an ink pen to a lap top computer.

What are the processes of writing? If we look at what professional writers do there is a wide variety of approach. Some believe in very detailed planning before starting to write, others reach for the pen or switch on the word processor and get stuck in. Still others plan a bit, then tear up the plans and write whatever comes into their heads.

If there is one thing that all writers have in common it is that they are prepared to go through a number of drafts before they get to the one they are prepared to submit. There are very few professional writers who can make do with the one draft; constant polishing is required by most. James Joyce used to think he'd done quite well writing half a page in a day with constant drafting and redrafting but then not that many of us try and write *Ulysses* and take over several years to finish it! We should make a distinction here between writers of fiction-novels, short stories on the one hand and writers of non fiction such as journalists, text book and report writers on the other hand. For the purposes of this book we will concentrate on the needs of the non-fiction writers although some of the advice will be applicable when you come to write that novel or short story which you feel is there somewhere deep inside you!

We start this advice with something that was written some years ago and which we have already mentioned, it is a book we would thoroughly recommend you to read since it is one which has had enormous influence on writers since it was first published in 1948.

Plain Words

The author, the late Sir Ernest Gowers, recommended the advice given to the staff of the Inland Revenue Department:

> There is one golden rule to bear in mind always:that we should try and put ourselves in the position of our correspondence, to imagine his feelings as he writes his letters, and to gauge his reaction as he receives ours. If we put ourselves in the other man's shoes, we shall speedily detect how unconvincing our letters can seem, or how much we may be taking for granted.

If we make allowance that his text may seem a little sexist for today's reader, his but not her, the advice is sound and it applies to almost every kind of communication not just as in this case sending letters. We saw the benefit of this advice when we looked at presentations and negotiating.

Your readers

We outlined key points relating to knowledge of one's audience in chapter 3; any writer should take time to think very carefully about the nature of his or her readership. It is easy to do this at the start of a piece of writing, to have this audience in your mind in line 1 paragraph 1 but it is also easy to lose sight of them as you get to page 12 of your text.

The first question that you as a writer have to answer is: who is my reader or readers? Behind this simple sounding question is a whole set of others needing to be answered. These could include:

- What do they know about this subject?
- How technically expert are they?
- What is their competence in English?
- Is English their second language?
- What expectations can be made about their previous reading/study of this subject?
- How will they be using this material? For instance, will it be a main text or will it be subsidiary to others?
- How are they likely to be reading this? Will they skim the contents and go for the conclusions? Will they be interested in the detail?

The more we know about our readers the more it can make our writing task easier, this is particularly true when it comes to pitching the material. There are other equally important questions that need to be asked and answered. Before reading on please make a list yourself

Those questions you need to ask and have answered

Following on from these observations we move into a form of assertiveness! It is being assertive to ask questions if you are in any doubt as to the writing task that you are being set. You need to be able to ask and have answered the following questions:

Why write this text?

In other words is there a suitable alternative? We've already noted the importance of this question in our section on meetings, pages 69 – 70. It is a crucial question in all communication tasks when we calculate the costs — direct and opportunity (i.e. what you could be doing if you weren't writing this report?)

Why write this text now?

Would there be a better time to do it? How does the writing of this report fit into current business planning, the pattern of meetings and presentations to clients?

Who is the audience or audiences?

We' ve already looked at this important question on the previous page. Remember though you may be writing for audiences — plural — a technical as well as a non-technical group. You may have to appeal to a group who are very IT familiar and in the same document appeal to others who are not. What is the answer? Well, you could supply an annexe to the report which is written for specialised readers; you could supply a summary in plain English for those non specialists.

What's the remit for this text?

This is perhaps one of the most important questions to be asked; it's already come up a number of times in this book, particularly when we were preparing to give our presentation. You should never start a writing task, any communication task, unless you have clarified the remit, that is the scale of the task, what you are supposed to cover and what weighting you should adopt. This refers to the balance of work you should put in to particular parts of your remit i.e. more effort in the statistical analysis and less in the background and overview. This issue must be clarified before you begin.

What else has been written on this subject before?

You certainly don't want to waste your time doing a lot of preparatory work only to hear from one of your colleagues in the staffroom that Burt did something like that a few months previously. What a pity!

When's the deadline for this text?

It is absolutely essential that a) you get some information about this and b) try and negotiate the best possible timing for your needs. As in all project management, and this is certainly that, you need to be able to work backwards from your goal. With a large report or similar project it would be worthwhile drawing up a planning chart as on the lines of Table 14.1.

   The more massive the task the more such planning charts are essential. You must keep a firm eye on deadlines; this is not some sadistic exercise, there is considerable merit in having such targets. Most writers admit that without such they would not be able to complete their work, drift sets in, you put off writing that draft, 'It can wait' you say, procrastination and so to doomsday!

Sept 25-30		Oct		Nov		Dec 1st		Dec 10th	Dec 17
clarify remit	initial outline	obtain data	more detailed outline	rapid first write-up	check with remit	first draft	proof read	second draft	final copy
✔	✔	✔	✔	✔					

Table 14.1

What's the format of this text to be?

This refers to the look of the document, how the print is supposed to be set out on the page or electronically on the screen. You will need to ask about such matters as print size (the pointage) print type — the typeface, length of line, width of margins, spacing between lines, placing of illustrations, use of headings and footnotes etc.

If there is no house format then you will need to make up a page and submit it to some of your readers/colleagues for their approval and suggestions. Research into readability suggests that the print size should be between 11 – 13 with larger size 14/16 for headings and that you should adopt one of the standard fonts such as Times, New Century Schoolbook etc. Avoid fussy 'artistic' typefaces for your general text; these can distract your reader. Try to have reasonably wide margins so that the text doesn't look too cramped.

What's the house style for this text?

It is important to know whether you should adopt the impersonal third person:

The materials were collected and tested.. (passive)

or is it permissible to write in the first person:

I collected the materials and tested them to... (active)

In general, most reports and documents will be written in the third person using the passive. A personal style may however be appropriate if:
• The writer is an expert and is giving his/her view
• Has been provided with a personal remit
• It is a personal investigation.

For more information on style and the uses of the active and passive see page 130.

Questions on copyright and confidentiality

These questions must be answered before you begin. There's little point in embarking on a major writing task if much of it will have to be re-written to escape problems of confidentiality or copyright.

The actual writing process

Writing is a very personal process and what we outline here are some suggestions which might help if like many others you get stuck and find deadlines passing with awful predictability.

You may find it helpful; to draw up a rough outline before you commit yourself to the actual writing up. Take a large sheet of paper and a pencil and just sketch out the various components of the report and how they might link together. At this stage this is very much a outline and not a fixed plan; you may well want to change it as you go along. An example is shown in Table 14.2.

As you map out your outline think of some kind of logical sequencing for your material — that is logical to your reader! A report should be accessible; your reader should be able to see where you are going; the material shouldn't be laid out in some kind of haphazard brainstorm! Your arrangement might be along the lines of:
- Most important topic to least important (VIP-> LIP)
- Grouping of material in terms of what belongs to what
- Sequencing of some kind — time/process bound etc.

As you outline consider where the best place would be for any graphics. This is where storyboarding can be very helpful. it is a technique for expanding your outline into a section by section visualisation of the material. You are best to use large sheets of paper, for example, flip chart sheets, and on each sheet place:
- The main theme of the report/document
- The section number
- The various sub themes
- The key graphics that you wish to make use of.

You can build these up by sticking various drafts on to them/alongside. Pin them up

---

1st Outline

Intro/background	....
Data collected	....
Method	....
Discussion	....
	....
	....
	....
Conclusions	....
Recommendations	....
Appendix	....

Table 14.2.

---

on a wall so that the whole document can start to take shape before your eyes. By doing this you will be able to integrate text and illustrations.

Report
Introduction
....
....
....
Development
....
....
Conc
....
....
Recs
....

Table 14.3

You will be able to see at a glance whether for instance your findings do tie in with your conclusions and your conclusions do in fact come naturally from your recommendations (see Table 14.3).

It may be that as you write up then you'll find you need more graphics. As a general rule it is better to have a few really useful graphics which complement the text and help your reader see what it is you're doing than a whole lot just put in for effect and as a space filler!

Going for it

Once you've collected your 'data' and you've drawn an outline then we suggest you 'go for it'. This means that you write or word process (write if you can only two finger type) a first draft. We suggest that it is often better to write it; this way you have the various sheets laid out in front of you; with a word processor it is so very easy to loose track of where you are in the argument — you need to take hard copies and keep scrolling down to find where that particular point started and how it leads to the next.

Do this rapidly and do not stop to check on spelling. Make an estimate for the spelling, put a '?' against the word and look it up later. If you stop in mid flow and look the word up in a dictionary or on your spell checker then you may well lose the thread of what it is you're writing. You can do the spell checking and proof reading later. Aim at this stage to get a draft down on paper. Don't keep putting it off. Motivate yourself with rewards — that cup of tea and chocolate biscuit when page 3 is finished; that visit to the pub when you've reached page 8!

Don't throw away the first scribbled draft — it may be the best you'll do — not in accuracy of English but in flow and in quality of thinking.

Edit and edit

When you got that draft then you will need to do some editing. This is a process whereby you cut and polish the draft until it is where you want it to be. Here is an example of editing. If you look back to the beginning of this section you will notice the opening paragraph. Compare it with the first draft:

> For many people writing is the most difficult part of communication since they may have negative memories of school when they were told off by English teachers, their work commented on with 'Must Do Better!' Their confidence may not be helped at work by

having managers who peer over their shoulders to sample their writing or checking the quality of their work. Few of us can write under such observation.
The second draft with several edits:

- 2 sentences at the start of the paragraph rather than the long one
- the addition of 'pages covered with red ink' to make it more emphatic
- having 'a manager' singular rather than managers
- changing 'very few' for 'few' and 'scrutiny' for observation.

> For many people writing is the most difficult part of communication. They may have bad memories of school when they were told off by English teachers, of seeing pages of their work covered in red ink with the comment 'Must Do Better!' written underneath. Their confidence may not be helped at work by having a manager who keeps peering over their shoulders to sample their writing or checking on the screen the quality of their work. Very few of us can write well under such scrutiny.

And so to the third and final draft.

> Writing, for many people, is the most difficult part of communication. They often have bad memories of their English teachers, of seeing their written work covered in red ink with the ominous words "See Me' written underneath. At work, their confidence may not be helped when managers peer over their shoulders at their screens and check the quality of work on them. Very few of us can write well under such scrutiny.

Here in this third and final draft the words order has been changed, the word ominous has been included; the grammar has been changed from 'having a manager who keeps peering over their shoulders' to when managers peer over their shoulders at screens'.

You may prefer the first or even second draft, the author went for the third. You might like to have a go yourself!

Editing will seldom, if ever, take the text exactly where you want it to be but time is limited and you have other things to do. So the time will come when you've got to stop editing and give it a thorough proof-read before printing the final copy.

Check and Check again

Before handing in do proof read the text. Never rely on spell cheques! All they can do is to locate the word in their dictionary — if it's/*its* there/*their*/they're or passed/*past* — the best spell checker can't help you. So for these kinds of words and for all the an/*ands*, too/*to*/twos then you will need to proof-read — that is check it with your own eyes (it's a good idea to borrow a colleague's eye as well — ask him or her to look through your text; you'll probably be amazed at all the mistakes you've overlooked and amazed by how many drinks they want as reward)

Proof reading

Try this little proof reading exercise. Take a pencil and paper and see just how many errors you can spot. Remember proof reading is not just about spotting the spelling mistakes, it's also about checking punctuation, inconsistencies in usage etc, etc.

The occurence of a misspelled word in print is totaly unacceptable. The affect is disastrous an embarrassment to the printer, a distraction to the reader and a slur on the writers competence. Misspelling is a a sign that the role of the proofreader has been slighted or misunderstood, Although the proof-reader is principly committed to see that the proof follows the copy accurately,there is further committment to prevent the author, editor or or printer from looking rediculous. a proofreader is never presumtous, in correcting and incorrect spelling. Let no conscientious proofreader wholey acquiesce to the rule of the 'fellow copy" in regard spelling

How many errors did you spot? (The spelling errors are indicated in bold).

The occurrence of a mis-spelled [1] word in print is totally unacceptable. The effect is disastrous, an embarrassment to the printer, a distraction to the reader and a slur on the writer's competence. Mis-spelling [2] is a sign that the role of the proof-reader [3] has been slighted or misunderstood, Although the proof-reader is principally committed to see that the proof follows the copy accurately,[4] there is further commitment to prevent the author, editor or printer from looking ridiculous. A proof-reader is never presumptuous [5] in correcting an incorrect spelling. Let no conscientious proof-reader wholly acquiesce to the rule of the 'fellow copy' [6] in regard to spelling. [7]

[1] mis-spelled — the choice of hyphen is up to you, but if you do decide to hyphenate then be consistent and use it throughout the text. The same would apply to proof-reader. Mis-spelled can also be spelt mis-spelt. Many words in English have more than one spelling e.g. focusing or focussing. The important thing is to be consistent in use as in [2] and [3].
[4] Remember to check spaces after punctuation: single space for commas, normally double for full stops.
[5] There is no need to use the comma here; it is not helping the sense, removing ambiguity or adding emphasis — the most obvious ways of using commas.
[6] Watch out for inconsistencies in the use of inverted commas: avoid using 'and' together round a word or phrase.
[7] Do watch out for missing full stops at the end of sentences.

We now move to particular forms of writing: the report, the letter and memo and the article.

Specific types of writing

In the previous chapter we examined some general issues relating to writing, in this one we provide specific advice on such matters as writing a report, handling letters and memos.

Reports

No one really likes writing reports, although to produce one that actually is read and taken notice of can be very satisfying (and very exhausting!). The following advice is designed to help you write reports which are taken notice of, i.e. they are read, and fully digested.

The writer of 'successful' reports has to bear in mind the needs of the readers of the text. In this respect the task is very much as we outline in the chapter on presentation skills — keep your audience very much in mind. They are both examples of good customer care. If you don't bother with your readers' needs why should they bother reading your work?

What is a report?

A report can range from 1 to 1000 plus pages . It is one of the most important means by which you will communicate the results of your work or that of your group or section.

A report is a structured text with headings and sub headings. It is designed to be read quickly and easily. It should look like Figure 15.1 to your reader:

But not like Figure 15.2 — all text and no headings, therefore so much more difficult for your busy reader to grasp. Your reader, you hope, will start at the beginning and work his or her way through the text, but readers are perverse, they sometimes start with the appendix and go on to the introduction. Sometimes they read one line and skip 20 pages to find another. They may only be searching for a few paragraphs. It is our job to assist them skim and scan, although we do hope we can 'seduce' them into giving

---

Title

1. Intro

....
....

2. Method

....
....

3. Findings

....
....

4 Conclusions

....
....

5 Recommendations

....
....

6 Appendix

....
....

Figure 15.1

our hard read that close read which it deserves. That's why we should avoid presenting them with this:

Title

No one really likes writing reports, although to produce one that actually is read and taken notice of can be very satisfying (and very exhausting!). The following advice is designed to help you write reports which are taken notice of, i.e. they are read, and fully digested.The writer of 'successful' reports has to bear in mind the needs of the readers of the text. In this respect the task is very much as we outline in the chapter on

---

A report normally has:

An introduction — this sets out what the report is about and why it has been written — its purpose and scope. It might also provide an overview of other work carried out on the same subject.

> This report analyses the...
> The purpose of this report is to investigate causes of the...

(In longer reports and dissertations this is normally a separate section and is entitled *Literature Review*.)

A background section. This seeks to place the reader in the scene. Writing a background presents very real difficulties. We must know who are readers are otherwise it is so difficult to pitch it appropriately. In general a background should be:
* concise
* relevant
* unbiased — i.e. we do not wish to 'contaminate' our readers into one way of thinking before they've had the opportunity to discover the material for themselves and make up their own minds from the evidence presented.

Method section — this should indicate the manner by which you gained the data, the way in which you analysed and sorted the data (the experiments carried out, the statistical methods used etc.). The test for this is: could someone reading this repeat the experiment by simply reading what you have written. If not then you have not made your working sufficiently clear! E.g.

> The data was analysed using a coefficient correlation; this ...

> The opinions of staff were obtained by using a questionnaire (see appendix 1) and by the use of two focus groups (see appendix 2 for details).

The *Discussion or findings* section. Here you comment on the results and discuss the various findings. E.g.

> There were indications that the move towards Investors in People (IIP) has sharpened attitudes to training. This was apparent throughout the organisation.

Conclusions. Here you draw together any outcomes that emerge from this discussion of your findings. Sometimes the conclusions will leap out; at other times you will only be able to present very cautious conclusions that will require further work to prove or disprove them. E.g.

> From these results, it is concluded that the combination of internal training with the occasional use of outside specialists does provide a good base for further customer care..

Notice that most reports are written in a certain style — the passive. We examined this on page 123 but to recap, if we write 'It is concluded' as opposed to the active 'I concluded' it is because we wish to highlight what has been done rather than who has actually done it.

In the sentence *I analysed all concentrates of potassium,* the emphasis falls on the subject I. But are we as readers that interested in the person who carried out this experiment? Not usually, unless we wish to closely study their methods, e.g. 'Show us how you did it Professor — explain your technique!' Normally we want to know what happened — in this case that the concentrates were analysed.

Recommendations. Not all reports have recommendations. You as a writer might feel that you have not had enough time over the investigation, have not been able to explore deeply enough or gain enough experience of the organisation/system you are researching to be able to write recommendations. Suggestions or Ways Forward may then be more appropriate.

If you do write recommendations then remember they must be firmly linked to your findings and your conclusions; they can't appear from nowhere. Remember also that you will help your readers if you can provide them with some idea as to the priority behind this list of recommendations: priority as in:

- *Cost*: the most expensive to the least, or vice versa
- *Time*: the one that can be done quickly to the ones which will require time for completion
- *Complexity*: the easiest to achieve to the most complex.

Before starting

We listed the questions that need to be asked before we started the writing process. Nowhere is this more important than before commencing a report. There's absolutely no point putting pen to paper, finger to keyboard or plotter to graph until you have found out:

- The remit?
- Who's going to read it?
- What's it supposed to look like — the format?
- When it is supposed to be handed in?

Getting started

We examined on pages 125 – 126 various ways of writing. For reports we suggest that you do seriously consider drawing up an outline before you commit yourself to the actual writing up. There are various ways of doing this.

For instance, take a large sheet of paper and a pencil and just sketch out the various components of the report and how they might link together. At this stage this is very much a outline and not a fixed plan; you may well want to change it as you go along (Figure 15.3).

As you map out your outline think of a logical sequencing for your material — that is logical to your reader! A report should be accessible; your reader should be able to see where you are going; the material shouldn't be laid out in some kind of haphazard brainstorm! Your arrangement might be along the lines of:

- Most important topic to least important (VIP-> LIP)
- Grouping of material in terms of what belongs to what
- Sequencing of some kind — time/process bound etc.
- Moving from familiar to unfamiliar

As you outline, consider where the best place would be for any graphics. It may be that as you write up then you'll find you need more graphics. As a general rule it is better to have a few really useful graphics which complement the text and help your reader see what it is you're doing than a whole lot just put it for effect and as a space filler!

If you don't like the outline method then you might like to draw yourself a tree diagram, each branch represents a possible topic and how they 'hang' on the tree will determine their placing in the overall structure.

Example of a short report:

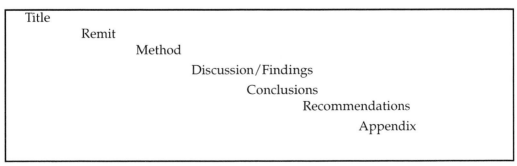

```
Title
        Remit
                Method
                        Discussion/Findings
                                Conclusions
                                        Recommendations
                                                Appendix
```

Figure 15.3

You could also use a brainstorm technique similar to the one we recommended to start for planning for a presentation or some kind of flow chart system.

Going for it
Once you've collected your 'data' and you've drawn an outline then as we suggested on page 125, you should 'go for it'.

Check and Check again
Before handing in do proof-read the text. Remember never rely on spell cheques!

Write a summary
A summary is an overview of the report. Within a paragraph or two it should provide your reader with the essential of the report. The test of a good summary is: after reading it can he or she now understand what the report is all about (not the detail) but the main idea. If the answer is NO then you will have to make your summary clearer and perhaps add a little more detail to it.

In some cases you will be asked to write an abstract. This is a summary of a summary. It is usually no more than 10 lines, 100 – 150 words and puts into a nutshell what the report/document is all about. It contains the key words which can, when entered into data base be used to retrieve the text.

Add an appendix
Use this for all the detail that you do not need in the main body of your report. E.g.

Replies to the questionnaire (see appendix) indicated...

If the material is important put it in the report since few people ever read appendices unless they are particularly interested or suspicious. (What's he hidden?)

Add a title page with your name, date and main/sub title in bold print.
See Figure 15.4.

The Chemistry of Real Porridge

Report

James Hardy Stir

Handed in Wed 31st Sept 2000 to Prof. O.L.D. Salt

Figure 15.4

- Number each page and bind it so that the pages won't come loose.
- Hand it in before the deadline!
Example of a short report

Here is an example of a short report. Consider how it is written. What changes would you make to it? Do spend a few moments on this exercise before you read our suggested changes.

Possible Housing Developments
Hillside Borough Council

The Planning Committee of Hillside Authority has had three meetings to discuss the following matter and a number of reports have been received from the Surveyor and the Legal Department re Greenside.

The Legal Department reports that there are no restrictions, i.e. no rights of any kind and no encumbrances that would prevent building. But the site does have some problems. It is a triangular block and this would mean that those houses built close to the apex will have much smaller gardens than those on the other side. We understand too that a few of the contractors in the town are not busy and we should expect some competitive tenders in the near future.

Consequently we do suggest that the Council should proceed to find out what grants will be available and what the cost of building would be by taking some provisional tenders.

The site (near Greenside) does seem to be suitable for building and all the indications are that it would take two or three-storey houses. We have been informed by the water, gas and electricity authorities that three services are all readily available. We would recommend therefore that the Council proceeds and decides to build here because we have heard that private developers are interested in the site.

Here are our criticisms do you share them?
- The title is vague (what kind of housing, where, whose, when? There are no sub titles to help direct the reader's attention. Remember that your readers will want to make their way through the text in the way that is important to them. Signposts in the way of titles can be immensely helpful.
- There is very little cohesion in this text. Cohesion is about how the text sticks together and how the reader is carried forwards from point to point and from paragraph to paragraph. For instance, if we examine the start of para 2 it looks as though that paragraph will be mainly about the legal department's view of this proposed development; however, as we read we notice that we get into gardens and site considerations, very much the same as is discussed in paragraph 4.
- The recommendations are buried in the final paragraph; these should be set out as a separate heading so that the reader's eyes can be rapidly drawn to them. Remember the recommendations might be the main target for some of your readers.

Here is our suggested re-write of this report. Does yours look like this?

Proposed Housing Near Greenside Meadows

Introduction

The Planing Committee of Hillside Borough has been asked to report to the Council on whether or not an estate should be built near Greenside Meadows.

The Committee has had three meetings to discuss this matter and a number of reports have been received from the Surveyor and the Legal Department.

Legal Considerations

Our Legal Department reports there are no restrictions, i.e. no rights of any kind and no encumbrances that would prevent building.

The Site

There are some problems: the site is triangular and this would mean that those houses built close to the apex will have much smaller gardens than those on the other side. But this is not a major drawback and it does seem possible to build two or three-storey houses. We have been informed by the water, gas and electricity authorities that these services are all readily available.

The Contract

We understand that a few of the contractors in the town are not busy so we should expect some competitive tenders.

Conclusion

We would recommend that the Council proceeds and decides to build here because we have heard that private developers are interested in the site.

We thus suggest the following steps:
- The Council should find out what grants may be available.
- The Council should ask for tenders at the earliest opportunity.

15 April 2000

J Hardie
Chairman Housing Committee

This draft does provide the reader with a more meaningful title, the sub headings are designed to guide the reader's eyes through the text (Always remember that some of your readers may only be interested in one section of the report so do your very best to help them find it).

We have tried to group like with like, i.e. law with all legal issues, site with all site issues as opposed to the original draft where topics where scattered around and the text had little by way of cohesion — sticking togetherness.

The longer report

Let's look at the longer report. Here is the material that forms the report. We invite you to draft your own version before you see what was done by the report writer, then you can criticise the result.

Read the following case study and compile a short (approx. 1.5 – 2 pages) report. Supply

- Title
- Remit – introduction
- Findings with various headings
- Conclusions
- Recommendations

We do suggest that you draw yourself and outline, a tree diagram, or a flow chart before you actually start composition.

The situation

Jill Smart is an Investors in People Assessor. She has recently completed a survey of Hazel Nut a small charity which specialises in assisting young children with learning difficulties. Here is a summary of her findings. Using these please complete a formal report with headings for the managers of the charity.

Material for the report:

Very enthusiastic senior managers for IIP aims. Real commitment. Records of staff training kept up to date. These show evidence of structure and planning. Much improved since interim visit. Spoke with Chairman of trustees. No training planned for Trustees — this was specifically noted in interim report. Action required.

Interview with sec/receptionist — she appeared not to be aware of IIP and seemed vague about any training she had received. This is disappointing considering the managers' enthusiasm for IIP. It raises some disquiet about communications between staff and managers.

Written plan identifying organisation's training needs well organised and shows good measure of planning. However some doubts about specific actions to be taken. Good on broad areas but needs to be strengthened in detail — specifically it needs to show better sequencing of training. Disappointed to see that training & development objectives not clearly linked to external standards — NVQs etc. Would recommend further work on this. Interview with computer operator — evidence of induction did not match up with agreed induction plans as set out by organisation. Some discrepancy here.

Attended team meeting between managers and staff — positive atmosphere. Well chaired. Previous minutes of such meetings did not reflect training and development issues. Need to note these more clearly. Doubts concerning the quality of communication between trustees and management of charity. Strongly recommend that more managers attend such meetings and that Training & Development was more regularly placed on the agenda of such meetings. Minutes of such meetings could do with expansion — rather bald at present.

Strongly suggest more be done to improve communication between Charity and its client groups. A review of such links was promised by the end of 1996 but little progress seems to have been made. Urgent! Trustees' own training and development not actioned despite suggestions from external IIP consultant. Would strongly urge moves in this direction. A number of companies do run courses in Strategic Planing etc. and would welcome attendance from a small number of Trustees. Local TEC would reimburse 50% of costs.

Some work been done on costs of training and staff development. Much improved budgeting but refinements and improvements needed. Suggest obtaining help from local TEC consultant. 50% of costs would be met General recommendation: award to be withheld until these specific points attended to. Suggest next assessment in 6 months time.

Here is the final report as submitted by Jill. List what you feel are its strengths and state how, given the material she had to work on, it could be improved. We have not included the appendix.

Investors in People Assessment
Report on Hazel Nut
Jill Smart IIP Assessor Feb 15th 2000

1. Introduction
The purpose of this report is to assess the suitability of Hazel Nut for the IIP Award.

2. Background
Hazel Nut is a small charity (11 staff) which specialises in assisting young children with learning difficulties. This report summarises the findings of a survey carried out by IIP assessor Jill Smart during the week 16 – 21st Nov 1999. The survey consisted of interviews with staff, managers and trustees, attendance at staff meetings and discussions with external clients. (see appendix for details).

3. Findings
Trustees — having spoken with the Chairman there appears to be no planned training for Trustees. An interim report (Feb 1998) specifically noted this matter. This issue needs to be addressed.

Staff — Senior management at Hazel Nut are very enthusiastic about the aims of IIP and demonstrate real commitment to these. Staff training records are kept up to date and show evidence of structure and planning. This is an area which has much improved since the interim visit.

There is also a written plan which identifies the organisation's training needs this is well organised. This plan requires strengthening in terms of specific actions and would benefit from a more detailed sequencing of training.

An area which requires further development is that of linking training and development objectives to external standards such as NVQs.

Additionally, there appears to be a discrepancy between the induction plan set out by the organisation and the actual induction training given to staff. This was revealed by an interview with the computer operator.

Since the interim visit, the organisation has improved budgeting techniques in relation to costs of staff training and development. Refinement of these techniques needs to be activated.

4. Communication

4.1 Internal

One member of staff who was interviewed did not appear to be aware of the organisation's desire to achieve IIP status. This person was vague about what training she had received. This lack of awareness would suggest that communication should be improved between staff and their managers. This is particularly the case given the enthusiasm for IIP demonstrated by management.

The Assessor attended a team meeting between managers and staff at which a positive atmosphere was prevalent. The meeting was well chaired. However, minutes of previous meetings did not reflect training and staff development issues. It is suggested that these be more clearly noted.

Throughout this survey it was unclear as to what the quality of communication was between Trustees and Management.

4.2 External

The charity conducted a review in 1997 which recommended efforts to be made to improve communication between the organisation and its client group. To date this has not been carried out. Immediate action need to be taken on this.

5. Conclusions

5.1 While the management of the organisation is very enthusiastic about the aims of IIP and is fully committed to attaining these standards, the problem areas identified in this report require resolution before any award can be made.

5.2 The problems identified relate specifically to training and development of Trustees and Staff, together with both internal and external communication issues.

5.3 If these problems can be addressed within the timescales given, there remains the possibility that the IIP award could be made following a final visit and report. It is suggested that this visit takes place in 6 months time.

6. Recommendations

6.1 Trustees be given training in **strategic planning**. The local TEC would be prepared to invest 50% of costs incurred.

6.2 Improvements to be made to **internal communication** between staff and managers. This should take the form of improved clarity in the way that minutes of team meetings are written up. In particular there should be direct noting of staff training and development issues. Training and development matters should be replaced more regularly on the agenda.

6.3 Managers should be encouraged to **attend meetings** more frequently.

6.4 **Communication links with client groups** need to be improved. Recommendations on this in the interim report should be carried through.

6.5 There should be **refinements to the budgeting** for costs of training and staff development. The local TEC could provide 50% of costs.

6.6 That a further and final assessment be carried out in 6 months time (Sept 2000) and **IIP accreditation be awarded** on condition that these specific recommendations are met in full.

Signed

Jill Smart

What are the merits of this report? What did you think as you read it through and compared it, hopefully with your version? We could list these as:
- It is structured for rapid reading and assimilation — the use of headings and sub headings; the spaces between the paragraphs etc. The material is clearly set out and should appeal to the browser, the skimmer and well as those close readers.
- The purpose behind the report is clearly stated.
- The background is sufficient for the reader who is familiar with the situation; naturally a longer and more detailed background would be necessary if one was writing for an outside audience.

However, are you satisfied that the conclusions tie up sufficiently with the recommendations? Certainly one should never introduce new material in the recommendations section. This is a very important consideration. Are you happy with the use of bold in the recommendations? One could argue that if the recommendations are written clearly then there is no need for such embellishments.

2. Letters

Introduction

You will be familiar with letters — so many pour through our letter boxes each day. However because of their importance — and it might be that in these days of e-mail and the internet that the paper-based letter becomes of even greater importance — it's worth while taking the time to do to write them properly.

The word influence should be on your mind as you think of letters — and we are referring here to business letters for instance from professional to client. Naturally letters carry information but they do a great deal more: they also carry influence. A letter is part of your personal relations — your PR and marketing. Consider when you have read a letter from some organisation and it has been poorly produced, perhaps mis-spelled and difficult to fathom what the writer was getting at, what did it do for your estimation of that organisation? We suspect not a great deal!

Here's the opening of a letter that was given to the author — the name of the organisation has been changed for obvious reasons but the material in the text is genuine. What do you think of it as a specimen?

Dear Sir,

I write with reference to your correspondance dated 6th Feburary 2000 regarding your PC, as always I was very concerned to receive this type of letter from any customer.

I must firstly apologise for the delay in getting your computer to you, it was an extremely busy period before and just after the Christmas break. Certainly the sales team were working through the night so that we could honour our scheldues, however a small percentage of our customers did experience a delay such as yours for which the company is very sorry about. We enclose vouchers to help compensate for the inconvenience you have been caused in this matter.

Yours sincerely

Did you spot all the errors?
- Spelling of correspondence, February, schedules!
- Misuse of the comma for the full stop, 2nd line para 2
- The odd grammar, i.e. 'for which the company is sorry about', final line.

You can see the effect this would have on any reader. The aim of this letter remember is to apologise for a lapse in service; you would think that the writer would be on his or her very best writing behaviour. A well composed letter in response to a complaint which is correct factually, clear of all errors and adult in tone, can not only put matters right as far as the immediate complaint is concerned but also start the 'healing' process so that the reader gains an enhanced impression of the said organisation and may, just may, return as a customer, and even recommend it to friends.

Any letter written for the attention of one person may well get passed on to others, so that the paper, or electronic letter is an ambassador for you and for you and your organisation.

Have a go at re-writing this letter — the one that unfortunate customer wanted to receive as opposed to the one he actually did! Here is our suggested re-write.

Dear Mr X,

Late delivery of Personal Computer

Thank you for your letter of 6th February 2000. We are sorry that you experienced such poor service from us and would like to offer you our apologies.

Although the Christmas break is a very busy period for us, you should have received your computer by the 15th of January. We have since found out that your order was incorrectly filed with others; this explains the delay. We are very sorry this has happened. We have as a result of this error re-organised our system for recording orders.

To help compensate for this inconvenience you were caused, please accept the
enclosed vouchers which will entitle you to discounts off your next purchase from us.
We look forward to being of further service to you.

Does this revised letter provides the information, i.e. why the product did not reach the
customer and states that 'we are a good organisation to deal with even though we do
occasionally make mistakes, at least we learn from them and have the interest of our
customers firmly to heart!' You could argue that it is a little over the top in its apology
and that the final sentence could be removed with any loss.

Structuring your letter

The reason for supplying a clear structure in a letter is very much the same as we
stated earlier on reports; our readers want to get the gist of what we are about; they
want to be able to glance along the sheet of paper and be able to abstract the key ideas
without having to plough their way through a thicket of language.

One way we can aid our readers is by putting in bold at the top of the letter the
topic we are writing about. This normally comes after the salutation (the Dear Sir, Dear
Mrs Jones etc). We can by doing this also provide a very definite structure for our
subsequent paragraphs. Think **TRAP (Topic-Reaction-Action-Polite Close)**

T for TOPIC — our first paragraph after the title should establish exactly why we
want our reader to read our letter. In many business letters it is often one main topic
divided up into several sub topics.

It is important to read very carefully any pervious correspondence to establish what
exactly are the various topics that are needing to be addressed. You know how
infuriating it is when you have taken the time and trouble to compose a letter setting
out your views, your complaints etc. only to read the answering letter and find that
few if any of these points have in fact been answered. This is one of the problems of
standard letters — precisely because they are standard they cannot be flexible enough
to provide a satisfactory answer to many letters of request, complaint and inquiry.

Here is an example of setting out a topic in a letter. Do you think it clearly sets this
out? What changes would you make?

The Contracts Manager
Cut Up Rough Legal Advice Centre
Leeds

Dear Contracts Manager
You were kind enough to come to the Young Civil Engineers Assoc. of West Yorkshire last month. We very much enjoyed your lecture.

You did say that it might be possible to organise a follow-up visit to your firm to talk through with you and members of your team some of the particular issues that you didn't have time to cover in your talk. As Rep for the Young Civils I have been asked if it would be possible to arrange such a visit. We would be particularly interested in looking at some details of contracts with local government that you said were particularly awkward.

Would any of the following dates be suitable March 3rd, March 11th or March 15th. 2000. The late afternoon would suit us best.

Yours with best wishes.

Did the writer set out the topic clearly and concisely so that the reader can gain at a glance what he or she has to do ? Compare this possible re-write

Dear Contracts Manager

I am writing as representative of the Young Civil Engineers Assoc. West Yorkshire Department to ask you whether we could take you up on your kind offer you made after your lecture to us last month.
      You invited us to............

Do you feel this better sets out the topic — the intention of the letter ?
      R this stands for your response. Having made sure that you send a clear signal to the reader that you have understood the position then you will need to spell out exactly what kind of actions you and your organisation propose to take.
      A stands for action. Sometimes these two paragraphs or parts of the letter would be joined together, i.e. the response is the action. However there may be a separate response section. The important point is that this is the stage where you set out the action or conclusion so that your reader can be in no doubt what is to happen. Such phrases as: 'we intend'; 'therefore we can now'; 'we are prepared to offer you', etc.
      P stands for the polite close. No matter upset an annoyed you are with your correspondent this must not show. Keep cool. Use this part of the letter to re-assure your reader: 'If there is anything further I can help you with please don't hesitate to contact me on...'
      We are not saying that this structure can be applied to all situations, for instance it might be possible to move from Topic to Action without any consideration of response. Here then is a complete letter written to this structure and in reply to the letter we

quoted earlier. (Note we don't usually put TRAP down the side of the letter, this is for demonstration purposes only).

Dear Dave Brown

T   **Follow-Up to Lecture on Engineering & Contract**

R. Thank you for your letter of February 13th. I should be very pleased to welcome you and your colleagues to our company.

A. I will expect you and your party outside the main gates at 4.30 pm. We shall then have a short tour of the plant. I have asked our site managers to join us and lead this . This tour should take approx 40 minutes. We can then offer you coffee and sandwiches before the talk at 5.30. We would expect this and any follow up questions to last about an hour so you can book your coach to collect you from the main gates at 6.30 – 6.45

P. Thank you for your appreciation of my talk. We look forward to you being our guests on Feb 13th. I've noticed in my diary that it happens to be a Friday so these timings might go slightly awry.

All best wishes to you and your colleagues.

Do you feel this is a well structured, clear and friendly letter?
Having looked at the structure we should now review the actual layout.

Layout of letters
The layout of your letter is designed to make the reading task easier for your reader. Basically there are 3 main standard layouts. Which one you will adopt will depend on the 'house style' of the organisation you represent or if self employed the one you have decided to use. (See page 143.)

Traditional (use this for any handwritten letters)

Your Address

Date

Reference
Reader's name & address

Salutation (Dear...)

Possible Heading

....

....

....

Body of letter (indented)

....

....

....

....

....

....

Subscription (Yours etc.)

Signature

Blocked

Your Name/ of Firm Address
Telephone/Fax/e-mail

Ref. & date

Reader's Name & Address

Salutation

Possible Heading

....

....

....

Body of letter (indented)

....

....

....

....

....

....

Subscription

Reader's/ Firm's name

Semi Blocked

Name of Your firm/Organisation
Address
Telephone fax e-mail

Date

Reference

Reader's name
Address

Salutation

Possible Heading

....

....

....

....

....

....

Subscription

Firm's name

Signature
Designation

Style in Letters

Layout and structure is reasonably simple compared with the complexities of style. The most important thing to remember is that the style should be appropriate to the situation, the context in which you are writing. E.g. Hi Bill. We examined this on pages 104 – 05. Remember that the culture you are working in will affect the style.

'Having a great time', is a most appropriate style for a post card but not for a business letter. Dear Sir would not be very appropriate if you were corresponding with someone in organisation you had developed some kind of on-going business relationship with.

Examine this opening to a letter. The context is that the recipient has recently been interviewed for a job and has failed to get it,

Dear Sir

It is regretted that the Board were unable to recommend that your name go forward for appointment. We thank you for your application.

We said in the introduction to writing that *tone* was very important when it came to all aspects of written text. In letters your reader will be reading between the lines and therefore it is very important to read the text as if in the position of your reader. Try and imagine to yourself how he or she would feel as they opened that envelope.

For instance there's no point in writing "We were very distressed to hear about the problem that you had with your electricity supply". If it is obvious to both parties and especially the reader that the quality or the service provided, the way they been connected and then checked left so much in terms of quality of performance that they couldn't be that distressed.

Here is a possible re-write of that letter of refusal

July 25th 2001

Dear Mr Thomas

Thank you for attending the interview for the Post of ...... on July 24th. We were impressed with your application but do not feel able to recommend your appointment to the Board. We realise that you will be disappointed. The choice was very difficult.

Thank you for your interest in the organisation. We wish you well with your future.

Selecting the appropriate tone is crucial. It takes us back to Mr Gowers and his wise words of advice from 1948: Put yourself in your readers' shoes! This advice is highly relevant whether you send a letter or compose it as an e-mail.

Specific issues in E-mailing

We can approach the whole subject of e-mailing from the sender and the receiver's point of view. Firstly, as receivers. We noted in the introduction that people at work were being deluged by e-mails. We have to find coping strategies. In a recent audit of a large organisation the author found many staff who had absolutely no method of dealing with the flood. E-mails were just dumped into a large folder called MISC instead of being prioritised and 'catalogued'. What is often required is a little training/coaching on how to make the best use of the office system which handles the e-mails It's all about having systems for retrieval that work and which can save time. When sending e-mails it is obviously vital that they are headed in a clear way so that the recipient will have some idea of what to do with them and where to file them. We also have to be very careful to whom we send the e-mails. There have been some notable cases in recent years where e-mails were broadcast to a wide audience with much embarrassment caused. Then as we have noted earlier in this chapter, we have to be particularly careful that we don't either start an e-mail war or contribute to it. If we receive an angry e-mail it is much better to sit on our reply and let our feelings cool before replying. In this example a frustrated and angry team leader had been e-mailed by his manager to get something done about travel requisitions. Feeling sore he banged off this e-mail to the team:

There have been a number of instances of late where Travel Requisitions have arrived on my desk after the required travel date. Let me make it quite clear to you all – no one can travel without prior approval from myself. Individual who bend the rules will not be tolerated and examples of such individuals will be made. So watch it.

This is an angry e-mailer! However this message, far from putting an end to the problem, only made matters much worse- his team took almost a perverse pleasure in handing in forms without prior approval. This. stimulated another shoal of even angrier e-mailing and counter e-mailing, which was neither efficient nor effective communication.

There are many issues relating to style of written English in e-mails. In general they are less formal than letters, however we have to remember Gower's advice and put ourselves in our reader's shoes. A style which is too informal can cause annoyance despite it being an e-mail. Suit the level of formality to the reader. The best advice is to take your tone and style from the sender's own. If you are initiating a communication then aim for the friendly and yet business like. It is certainly permissible to make use of dashes and other informal punctuation marks but do take care with spelling. Although e-mails are often composed at speed it is still good advice to check them before you 'ping' them away.

Writing for the screen

You may be asked to write an article for a website. Here are a few pointers to help you.

The first thing to remember is that your reader will be accessing this material off a screen and not on paper (unless he or she prints it out). Reading a screen is a very different challenge to reading a text on paper. Not so long ago it was predicted that the end of the book was nigh, that we'd all be reading off our computer screens, but this prophecy has proved as wrong as wrong can get. Bookshops are bursting at the seams with books, the publishers have never been busier.

The truth is obvious; people find reading from a screen a much less pleasant and a far greater challenge than reading from paper.

So if we're writing for the screen try to make this task as easy as possible.
• Don't use long lines; keep your margins wide
• Break up the text; space out the paragraphs and keep these short
• Make it crystal clear at the start what the text is about
• Use short subheadings to help guide the reader
• Avoid underlining- it might be confused with hyperlinks
• Use bold sparingly and don't use Italics (very difficult to read on screen as they 'swim')
• Use a sans serif font i.e. without 'curly bits' such as Arial – easier to read on screen
• Make use of colour but remember light tones – yellow, pink, green won't show up well.

Writing for journals

Professionals as part of their continuous personal development should be reading journals, they might also want to contribute to them. It is absolutely vital that you read and follow the instructions for submission of articles. Remember also that apart from main articles, journals are on the look out for short snippets, letters, reviews, work in progress etc.

Here for instance is a typical set of instructions (in summary) for submission to medical journals:

> Type/word process the manuscript double spaced, including title page, abstract, text, acknowledgements, references, tables etc. Each manuscript component should begin on a new page in the following sequence:
>
> - title page
> - abstract and key words
> - acknowledgements
> - references
> - tables (each table complete with title & footnote on a separate page)
>
> Illustrations should be of good quality, unmouted glossy prints, usually 127x173mm but no larger than 203 x254mm
> Submit the required number of copies of manuscript and figures in a heavy paper envelope. The manuscript should be accompanied by a covering letter, as described under submission of manuscripts and permissions to reproduce previously published material or to use illustrations that may identify human subjects.

Having read and understood the summary instructions you are then thoroughly recommended to read carefully the detail. Here for instance is the section relating to the title page.

> The title page should carry a) the title of the article, which should be concise and informative; b) first name, middle initial and last name of each author, with highest academic degree(s) and institutional affiliations; c) the name of department(s) and institution(s) to which the work should be attributed; d) disclaimers, if any; e) name and address of the author responsible for correspondence about the manuscript; f) name and address of author to whom requests for reprints should be addressed or statement that reprints will not be available from the author; g) sources(s) of support in the form of grants, equipment, drugs, or all of these; and h) a short running head of footline of no more that 40 characters (count letters and spaces) placed at the foot of the title page and identified.

This will give you some idea of the care needed in submission of material (text or electronic) for serious professional journals such as in this example, the BMJ. Do not let this put you off. These are ground rules which have been agreed and as there is fierce competition to get published the editors know that such ground rules will be followed. Do check on the latest instructions from the editors. These are updatred regularly and may well have been changed from those quoted above.

If you are actively involved with research in your profession you should seriously think of getting published; not only is there immense satisfaction in seeing your work in print but you are contributing to the wider pool of understanding amongst your colleagues. And don't neglect those letters and snippets which editors are constantly hunting for. Consider such themes as:

- Changes in professional – client relationships
- Developments in communicating between professional and client (on going work on plain English for instance)
- Marketing your work to clients
- How the Internet is assisting continuous professional development in your field
- Mentoring systems for young professionals etc.

So what's stopping you — author?

Follow-up reading

C. Turk C and J Kirkman, *Effective Writing*, E & F Spon, 1992
G. Wainwright, *Report Writing*, Management Update, 1987
J. Van Emden and J Eastal, *Report Writing*, McGraw Hill, 1993

Creativity in your communication

You will come across those situations where you get stuck in your communications — there doesn't appear to be any way forward. You've probably experienced this kind of thing:

'I keep telling him and telling him but nothing changes.'
'She doesn't want to say anything and I'm desperate for news.'
'These meetings just go on and on — nothing ever gets decided.'

These statements represent deadlock; the various sides are stuck and there's none of that ebb and flow which we saw earlier was essential for effective communication.

What is needed here is a change in strategy; there's little point in soldiering on, hammering away if there is no progress. The Law of Diminishing Returns doesn't just apply to economics, it's very relevant to human communications as well.

If you do find yourself stuck in your communications, then be creative and think tactics. Before reading ours, think back to any time when you were in a communications 'hole' and had to dig your way out. What tactics did you make use of? Did they work? Why?

Here are our suggested tactics. How far do they compare with yours?

- ***Back off.***
In other words it's not worth your while going on with this communication. After a time the more effort you seem to put in the less 'reward' you seem to get out of it. It's time to cut your losses. Obviously you would only make use of this tactic if the communication was not that valuable to you — a loss of communication that would not matter much.

- ***Change the direction.***
Instead of hammering away at telling, start asking questions — less output more input. Very often a change in direction will provide a chance for the parties in the communication to find a way out of their difficulties. Turn yourself round, face the other way, see your communication from a different angle.

- ***Change the mood, the tone.***
You might soften it, reduce its intensity, make it quieter, less personal, less parental more adult. It can be the tone which is acting as a block to communication.

- ***Change the environment.***
Try moving the chairs around, draw down the blinds; move from a corridor to a room. The wrong environment can rob a communication of its life and vigour. Think of all those meetings that just died because the room was small and stuffy. In 1985 President

Reagan carefully prepared the cabin by Lake Geneva for his meeting with the then Soviet leader Gorbachev: the open fire, the comfortable armchairs, the pot of coffee, nothing was left to chance to ensure the right environment for the barriers between them to come down.

- ***Change your posture.***

If you are standing up, try sitting down; try moving closer. There's enough research into non-verbal communication and other aspects of body language to show that how you appear to the other person in terms of your gesture can determine the success or otherwise of your communication. We've examined (page 36) the crucial importance of adjusting our posture to encourage the other party in an interview.

- ***Change the language.***

Change the formality, make it more informal, less full of jargon; make it more human, use analogies, examples to bring it closer to your listener. Language should be a bridge and not a barrier.

- ***Change channels.***

If you're using visual aids, stop, turn off the machine, move forward and speak directly to the audience. If on the other hand you have been speaking directly to the audience then as a change move across to the OHP and put on a slide. In other situations, stop faxing and e-mailing and go to see the person face-to-face. We've seen how important face to face communication is; it seems to be even more important in these days of instant electronic communication.

- ***Change the pace.***

If you always provide instant replies cool it down, allow yourself time for pause and reflection; if you've been rather recalcitrant in replying then surprise that other person by replying straight away.

- ***Change your audience.***

You may find that you have been communicating with the wrong audience — the people who would really appreciate your message have been hidden from you. Carry out a review with whom you communicate.

These are some possible changes to your communication that you could think of making if you're in that stuck situation where you do not appear to be making any progress. These are all possible strategic moves (like a game of chess). There's no absolute certainty that any of these strategies by themselves will do the trick but remember that saying of the public speaker, 'If you're not hitting oil; stop boring'.

There's absolutely no point in just hammering away using the same old channel, the same old system, the same old or new technology. Let's now see how some of these strategies could be used in reality.

Scene 1

The Presentation is not going well; the audience are looking bored, there is a good deal of restlessness, the message is definitely not going home. The speaker drones on:

'As you can see in this next slide the budget forecasts clearly show that unless we can make savings on.......' Yawn, yawn.

But suppose he now changes tack. He switches off the OHP, comes forward to the audience and away from the podium and says.

'Now let me give you an example which I think will bring home the seriousness of our position. ...'

Now he has them listening; the bored look has changed (on most faces) to one of interest. His example obviously strikes home to members of this particular audience. His voice unadorned by the bright light and large screen necessary to the display of the OHP slides, comes as something of a change and a pleasant relief; the presentation now has an immediacy and an increased impact for the audience.

After he has completed his example he walks back to the OHP and selects 3 of the 7 remaining slides to develop the conclusion to this talk.

Scene 2

The appraisal interview. This is not going that well. The appraiser Mike has got stuck with the appraisee Harry, who has pretty well clamped up. The questions relate to Harry's performance in his job as team supervisor but it's like drawing teeth. 'God', thinks Mike, 'another 45 minutes of this'.

A change of strategy is obviously called for. There's little point in hammering away at diminishing returns. Mike moves his chair away and goes across to the coffee pot; he pours out coffee for two and offers one to John, he also passes across a packet of biscuits, as he does he asks:

'We don't seem to be getting very far. I tell you what, why not ask me some questions for a change. I'm sure you've prepared some.'

John thinks hard as he dunks his biscuit in his coffee.

'Well now you've mentioned it, I was going to ask about the future of my section, I mean will it stay together now that the Appleyard contract has been cancelled'.

A brief exchange of views takes place; the situation has been effectively transformed — the relationship has been improved. What was needed to break the logjam was a simple change of direction. The move to the coffee pot and the opening up of questions to the appraisee enabled that to start happening. The two 'players' had been caught up in the formal rules of the game — the appraisal. One of them had to break free of this restriction and to communicate in a more humane and informal fashion.

Scene 3

A meeting. There is silence round the table, all 20 people look down at their notes.

'Well', says the chair, 'who has any ideas as to how we could improve this situation?'

Silence

'No ideas? we really must come to some kind of consensus over this matter.'

Some one at the end of the table speaks up:

'Chair can I suggest that we break into smaller groups; with so many round the table it may be that individuals do not wish to put their views on record. I suggest that we break into groups of say 4 or 5 using different corners of this room, and then come together in plenary to pool our ideas.

The chairman asked if it was a good plan. The meeting thought that it was and they all went off in various huddles to 'buzz' away!

The groups processed all kinds of ideas and in the subsequent plenary discussion some kind of consensus emerged. It became a much more productive meeting; something tangible emerged. People had felt less shy of giving their opinions in the small groups of three and four rather than at the table with all 20 looking at them.

These three scenes illustrate the point: if you're stuck be creative and think strategy, alter direction if needed to get yourself and your colleagues out of a hole.

We can also apply this principle of creativity and change of tactic to other forms of communication, i.e. the written/text based forms. We saw in chapter 15 when we were looking at report writing that it is essential to be able to appreciate your audience's needs and to work hard to gain feedback from them.

If the feedback is poor, if it appears that your reports, memos, letters, documents are not getting through, not being read and attended to then 'stop boring', find another tack.

Scene 4

Susan in Sales and Marketing has been sending a monthly report to her manager on her performance. This has been on going for some time. Susan has never received much feedback from her manager, apart from the occasional memo which starts: 'Keep up the good work', or 'Try harder next month'. This situation needs to be changed. Susan really deserves more feedback on her work.

What is needed here is a change of tactic, she should stop 'boring' and find another tack. She makes an appointment to see her manger after pointing out the amount of time that she spends on these reports and how she would like to receive more feedback. They settle down to think through a more cost effective and efficient process. The solution emerges as a summary report followed by a short meeting between the manager, Susan and her sales team once a month and after the manager has read her report.

The author, in carrying out communication audits, has come across situations where reports have been put together after a great deal of time and effort has been expended on them, sent off to the intended audience and then not attended to, filed, put away in drawers, used as stands for coffee mugs etc. — they go unread. It all represents a tremendous waste of time and effort not to say cost — direct and opportunity.

Inertia in our communication

The sub title of this chapter is 'getting out of a hole' One of the deepest holes in communication is that caused by inertia, a failure of will to try something different; just sticking to the same old formula, not willing to experiment, and not applying the basic laws of diminishing returns when the situation obviously calls for it.

So think strategically, refuse to become locked into a position. Put on your 'thinking hat'. For those of you who haven't come across De Bono's *Six Thinking Hats* (a book we would thoroughly recommend) then here's a very brief synopsis of his approach. It's based around the notion that we can all be more creative if we allow ourselves a chance to use the resources of our various thinking styles. These are the six hats (each hat represents a different thinking approach).

Red hat thinking: Wearing the red hat encourages thinkers to express how they feel about something, e.g. ordinary emotions like fear, dislike and suspicion and the more complex feelings in making judgements such as the well-known nurse's 'intuition' or the manager's 'hunch'.

Blue hat thinking: This thinking involves organising the thinking process, defining problems and shaping questions. With your blue hat on, you think of summaries and conclusions, monitor progress and ensure that rules are followed.

White hat thinking: This thinking deals in facts and figures, is logical and objective. It is neutral, offers no interpretations or opinions and is disciplined in approach.

Yellow hat thinking: This thinking is positive, constructive, optimistic and concerned with making things happen. There is a search here for values and benefits and a seeking out of opportunities to exploit them.

Green hat thinking: This is the creative hat. The colour symbolises the fertility and growth of seeds or ideas. The fundamental aspect of green hat thinking is the search for alternatives. It is this thinking hat which is most powerful in challenging the mindsets.

Black hat thinking: The black hat thinker points out what is wrong, why things will not work, what the risks are and what the dangers are. It is a devil's advocate hat. In a more positive sense it is the source of evaluation, constructive and critical thinking. Although creative thinkers often find black hat thinking destructive, in practice it can also be a source of challenging mindsets, i.e. that it is critical of stereotyped approaches to problems. It is particularly useful for teams to be aware of these hats. The author knows some teams where members have actually brought different coloured hats into the room and placed them on the table so as to remind each other of the principles of De Bono's advice.

There are many other ways of liberating our thinking. We would recommend Von Oech's 'Mental Locks and How to Break Them' approach. He suggests that we need to escape from typical locks to creative thinking. Some of these include:

It's not the right answer (but think of all those creative solutions that at first sight didn't look like a right answer: the mini car for instance!

That's not logical — well was the first computer mouse thought of as logical? We know that many thought it was a daft idea.

But that's not following the rules. Well, how many great inventors did that. Sorry Mr Brunel but your concept of an iron ship doesn't follow our rules.

But be practical. Think of how many great ideas that one's killed off!

Don't be foolish. You say you want some cardboard tubes, adhesive tape and that will save our Apollo 13 astronauts from carbon monoxide poisoning?

You can see the drift. We have to seriously challenge these mental locks, often set by others and often without any intention to stifle creativity, but their effect can be deadly.

By using these hats, avoiding mental locks and becoming more strategically minded in our communications we may well be able to get out of those communication black holes more easily. It's never going to be that easy in some cultures (see page 67) compared to others. Where there is empowerment, devolved authority and an open communication culture then getting out of holes will be that much easier; where there is an hierarchical, tightly controlling culture with little autonomy provided to staff then it will be that much harder.

The moral from all this is clear: avoid getting stuck. Each of your communications is different, every audience is slightly different (remember the analysis of communication styles we discussed on pages 11 – 12) A particular strategy that was effective with one 'client' might not work with another. Be creative in your approach.

This explains why we have placed such emphasis in this book on reflection and experiential learning. If you can spend some time after a success or failure in communication thinking as to why it went well or badly then you will be on the way to becoming that tactician we so recommend.

We realise that in some situations it is difficult to be 'creative' in your communications: set limits are laid down as to what you can and cannot do, initiative is severely curtailed. Our advice if you are in this situation is to point out the 'costs' ,your time for instance, of not changing tactic and the potential benefits of making changes for instance, through increased client satisfaction.

Successful communicators are seldom those who just have a set of skills, they also tend to be those who have some insight into situations and strategies that might fit a particular scenario. They also know how to be pro-active in making use of these to suit their particular needs.

References

E. De Bono, *Six Thinking Hats*, Penguin, 1985

R. Von Oech, *A Wack on the Side of the Head*, Penguin, 1995

Keeping up the progress

Coming now to the end of this book, for those of you who have been following it chapter by chapter we need to consider what should happen now. Reading a text on communication no matter how much it is geared to your needs, will only be at best a transitory experience — the print on the pages soon fades, the ideas cool, and the advice dims.

So how can you follow up this book and keep the advice alive? Here are some ideas.

10 ways of keeping up progress

1. Find a coach
Find someone who can work up your skills, rather as someone might help you improve your tennis, football, hockey, or guide you through the intricacies of the Advanced Driving Test. There are several important aspects to finding a coach:

The coach does not have to be an expert — merely competent in the communication skill/s you wish to develop. The greatest sports coaches are seldom experts themselves — they are often from the second flight of performers — highly competent but not international stars.

The coach must be someone whom you can trust and who can offer criticisms without fear or favour. For this reason we suggest that it is not your manager or team leader. Such people may well do some coaching with you but their position in authority can make it difficult for them to offer you the free range of suggestions and criticism that you really need. You may equally find it difficult to discuss in a completely open way your worries and doubts, especially in relation to your future career.

The coach must be someone who a) can observe carefully and b) communicate these observations in a clear way so that you, the person being coached, can understand and then put them into practice. The coach needs to be with you for some time so that he or she can monitor your progress.

We need to remember the difference between a coach and a mentor. Mentoring is not usually about skills development; it takes on a much wider nurturing and supporting role. A mentor relationship is about being there when advice is sought. For instance, a managing director of a firm may find someone in a similar capacity in a non competitor organisation who will act as his or her mentor. In this relationship there may be a small coaching element — working on one particular skill — but mentoring has this width of counselling, advice giving, and testing out of ideas carried through in a confidential way.

Example

A group of engineers have been asked to form a quality monitoring team. Harry has been elected convenor. He is unsure of his abilities to control the meeting of his colleagues. He fears that he keeps missing something important during the discussion. He realises that he is very unlikely to get much useful criticism from those sitting round the table, either they are too well mannered or find the business of giving feedback embarrassing, awkward and therefore probably best avoided.

However he does manage to find one member of the firm who has been convenor of a similar group some month previously and is prepared to come along and observe the meeting and act as his coach. At the end his coach sits down with him over coffee and offers this advice:

'John I felt you didn't include those at the end of the table nearly enough — it's very easy to forget this, OK? I also felt that during the second item on the agenda — budgets it was — you might have brought the discussion to a head rather earlier — it rather dragged on. We didn't actually get any clear cut decision. I saw John, taking the minutes, give you rather a worried look at that point; he was obviously unsure what had been decided. I used to find it very helpful to say something like: 'Right now to summarise where we've been on this item,' or words to that effect.

This kind of advice can be so important if our communication skills are to develop. Coaches are very useful because we can never see ourselves as others see us. We may feel that the meeting is being well chaired but only a coach who is actually sitting in the midst of the participants can see hear and 'feel' what is happening. Remember as we said several times in this book, what really matters is not what we think about our communications but the perceptions and feeling of those we communicate with. So do try and find yourself a coach. Even if you think you are highly competent you may benefit from having someone whose opinions you can trust provide comments to you.

2. Obtain feedback from your audience

We've noted several times in his text (for instance on pages 93 – 94) that successful communicators are able to tune in with their audience. One of the ways to do this is to be able to 'read' them. This 'reading' can be done in several ways: by looking at the non verbal behaviours, listening to the tone and tune of their voices and being aware of the nature of the questions asked (or the lack of them) etc. We saw in the section on report writing the importance of obtaining feedback from our readers so that we can re-tune or fine tune our product. If we don't get feedback or fail to recognise it when it comes, we may be fooling ourselves as to our success or otherwise.

3. Reflection after communication

We saw that the Kolb model of experiential learning provided us with a way of building from our experiences towards greater understanding (see page 3)

If after we have had a poor communication, one that gave us concern, embarrassment, anxiety, then we should spend some time reflecting on this experience in order that we could do it better. Similarly if we have had success in any communication — the presentation that went particularly well, that interview which really got to the heart of the difficulty etc. then again we should take some time to reflect on this success. If people do reflect after an experience it is usually those ones which were not successful, this is a pity since we should spend time on our successes. There's no point in being modest, if we really good at something we should recognise that we can use this success to build further good results or assist others in their development.

4. Observing others

We can learn a great deal about communication by becoming more aware of what others do; their styles, their approaches, the methods they use to get out of difficulties. You really never need to be bored again in meetings and conferences there is always someone to watch. By being observant you can pick up all kinds of cues as to tactics that can be employed. We are not suggesting that you can simply copy another person's communication style and make it your own, no that is not desirable — it will seem fake and others will see this as acting. It is much better to try and adapt another's style so that it will fit in with your personality and way of doing things.

5. Taking note of communication as seen TV, film and video and heard on radio or audio tape

We are not suggesting that you go around and deliberately model yourself on your favourite film star or TV personality, no but the media is full of examples of communication — successful and not so. There's a good deal to reflect on in these examples. If you want to hone your interview skills make a conscious effort to watch and perhaps video for further analysis, programmes such as the Frost Sunday Breakfast show. Listen to the Today programme on Radio 4 where the interviewers manage to extract a great deal of information from their guests in 3 minutes or less. Think of all those good lessons in communications learnt by those managers who went 'Back to the Floor'.

6. Reading

There's a huge list of books in print at the present which embrace every conceivable aspect of communication. From this vast number we have selected some which we feel will complement this book. One of the problems in looking for books on communication is that they very often do not have a very long shelf life and therefore the one you want may be out of print. For this reason we would recommend that you have a look in your public library and poke about second-hand shops. There is no one text which will provide you with all the answers. The list at the back includes general reading on communications as well as more specific texts on particular aspects such as presentation, interviewing and report writing. If you decide to become a serious student of communications then why not build up your own library, it will give you another excuse for going into second hand bookshops. Professional organisations will increasingly be making available on line information data bases to their members; from these you will be able to access a great deal of recent information and research on communications.

159

7. Practice

This is the way we most often develop skills. Remember though what we said about this in pages 7 – 10, practice by itself is seldom enough to enhance your skills by very much. You need to have feedback in the form of a coach, a video replay, photographs, evaluation from others such as comments from readers of your report etc. What tends to happen in all skills development is that you make some progress and then it tends to level off. This period may last some time and then you'll find things will improve, your progress will head upwards. The important thing is not to get depressed if this levelling out happens — it probably will.

8. Take courses

Reading this book and reflecting on your communication may have stimulated to go further and deeper. You could consider taking Open University courses; modules at local colleges, universities etc. There are also specialised courses in public speaking, report writing etc. run by the WEA, your local educational authority etc. If you work for a small firm where it would not be viable to bring outside specialist trainers you might be able to attach yourself to the courses run by larger organisations in your town/city/area. Very often they have a spare space due to cancellation/illness and you could for a fee join their group. This can be a very valuable way of meeting new people, networking as well as finding stimulation and enhancement your communication skills. If you've found this book helpful you can approach the publishers at Intellect <info@intellectbooks.com> to be put in touch with the author and his training programmes.

9. Take up some different but complementary activity

By this we mean have a go at debating, amateur dramatics, creative writing evening classes, calligraphy, yoga, the Alexander technique. Such courses can not only boost your self confidence but provide valuable techniques for presenting yourself and enhancing your interpersonal skills. That pottery class may make a real difference to your sense of self worth and confidence even if you never found much use for the strangely shaped pot!

10. Come back to this book again

How many of us have gone back to a book and found we had either missed sections or found that on a second or third reading we could understand more of the text.

Conclusion

We've travelled some way since the start of this book. What follows is a few pointers and reminders as to communication for professionals — the essential stepladder for career and life development. It attempts to summarise the essentials of the book in ten questions.

1) Is this communication really necessary?

We've posed this question many times in these pages. There's so much communication flying about these days, so much that gets thrown straight in the bin that we should ask ourselves at the very start:

Is this letter, fax, notice, e-mail, meeting, telephone call necessary? We're not saying that the occasional social telephone call/visit isn't a good thing but increasingly people are more and more time conscious and will resent their time being wasted. Remember it is not just the direct cost but the opportunity costs of the meeting etc. — what you could be doing with your time if you weren't attending!

So make sure that any communication is necessary and therefore is less likely to end up in a real or electronic waste-paper basket and that it doesn't clutter up your work time or that of others. The following questions are designed to help you towards that goal.

2) Is this communication targeted?

We've seen just how important this question is both in written and spoken communication. Just think how disappointing and frustrating it is when you tear open that interesting looking letter only to find that it has been misdirected and doesn't concern you at all. Or perhaps even worse when you open the envelope to find that some firm is asking you for money — an unpaid bill from way back — only to find after you've read the letter several times that the bill's not for you at all but for your neighbour, but it has your address on it!

So our first consideration when it comes to successful communication is — aim it at the right person/s.

The communication must hit the target to succeed if it is to have real impact.

It is so important for you to know who your customers are, their needs, not to mention important details like their names, designations (the jobs they do) their business & home address, telephone, fax numbers. e-mail numbers., Web site address.

Finding your key target customers and suppliers and keeping them in your sights is part of that detail. Neglect this at your peril. Successful communication in business is about how you build up and maintain a good relationship with customers, suppliers, getting one contract from a customer is fine but getting three or four every year for five years is what you need to be aiming at.

Good marketing can assist you in this targeting. But so can your own good sense and effective record keeping. With so many people moving in and out of jobs, taking part-time work, going on study leave, completing MBAs, travelling the world, etc, it is even more important for you to gather and update this information on your targets.

3) Is this communication timely?

Does your communication come at the right moment? There have been several examples in this book of communication coming at an inappropriate time. In most cases the advice should be: strike while the iron's hot! Don't delay. A rapid response will add a positive image to you and your organisation. Any delay might be thought of as a lack of enthusiasm, that you couldn't be bothered or that you don't have very efficient systems. On the other hand in some circumstances a delay may be very necessary and extremely desirable; it will provide you with that necessary reflection and pause for thought. Watch those angry e-mails!

Don't put off answering that letter or request for information. These small seedlings may grow into a substantial part of your future.

Don't neglect those opportunities for doing business which often present themselves on trains, planes and when sharing taxis!

4) Is this communication in the right language?

This has been one of our principal criteria in written language. We're not talking about you writing your leaflets in Chinese or making calls in Italian (if you can speak another language then take advantage of it). No we're referring to English. But which English?

Think of the times you've sat and scratched your head when trying to understand some bill from that building society, solicitor, etc. trying to work out what they mean in their special language. If only they could put this into plain English you've thought. Well, let us be sensitive and aware of the need to do this translation and explanation for our readers and listeners. At the same time we have to be very careful not to patronise our readers or listeners with simple language or Blue Peter tones!

5) Is this communication clear?

We've seen how a muddled communication often gives the impression that our actual work won't be that great. Sloppy communication often implies that a sloppy job will be done. The customer may well think, if they can't get that detail right then can I trust him over that other aspect of his or her work? We need to apply that famous test: put yourself in the position of your 'readers' and judge the results from their standpoint.

6) Is this communication accurate?

We've dwelt on this point several times. You may have had the unpleasant experience of your bank giving you the wrong information as regards your account. You go to the hole in the wall, enter your bank card and punch in your pin number and then stand back amazed at either how little you've got left or how much. Some have been known to have heart attacks on the spot.

It happens so easily — little mistakes which cause enormous problems, like the fact that no one apparently could find the binoculars for the lookouts on the Titanic so when they finally saw the iceberg it was too late to turn the ship! A simple mistake which had enormous consequences! So do get into the habit of checking and double checking your work.

7) Is this communication short and to the point?

Being concise was an important ingredient in spoken and written communication provided we didn't become terse and abrupt. Your reader or listener is usually busy; he or she will not want to plough through lengthy letters, reports or proposals, nor will your rambling phone call be welcome.

It's important to ensure that all our communication at work, with customers, suppliers and colleagues should be as concise as possible. However we should take care that it is not too short, then it can easily become abrupt and rude.

If the key material is put into a summary or abstract then we may want to provide for the users of our communication extra support in the form of supplementary materials, annexes, appendices etc. This may be necessary to re-assure them that we haven't skimped on the work.

8) Does this communication cover what it should cover?

As we aim to be concise we have to be careful to make sure that all the key points have been covered.

Isn't it frustrating to open that envelop and to find that only 3 of the 4 pages relating to the job that you are applying for has been enclosed, or part 1 of the quote is there but no signs of part 2. Even worse is the situation where the firm has at last paid up but inside the envelope believe it or not their cheque is only for half the amount due! So always check that what you do covers what you've been asked to do.

9) Will this communication get a response?

We've noted just how important this aspect of communication is. There's little point in just hammering away at communicating with people if you don't have a clue if anyone is actually receiving, listening and attending?

Effective communications is about checking that the message has gone home. This means taking trouble to find out if there is a response, and if there isn't one then asking for one — in the nicest possible way. You have probably been at the receiving end of those remarks:

> *Well I thought she'd understood that we have to scrap it.*
> *As you never said anything I thought it was OK to go ahead.*

So many problems in communication arise because we don't bother to get feedback/response to our message. We often assume that because the message has been sent then all is well. It is a very dangerous assumption, especially with the sending of emails.

Don't assume. Check.

10) Is this communication reasonable as far as its tone is concerned?

'It's not so much what you say, it's the way that you say it', we've seen what happens when we become 'parental' in our tone, how it can drive our respondent into a 'child' mode. It's so often the tone of voice in that curt tone of dismissal in the letter that leaves the listener and reader feeling cold, rejected and angry.

Tone of voice, tone in the writing can make a very big difference to how we understand and remember the communication.

Here then reduced to ten questions are some of the basic ingredients of all successful communication, themes which have run throughout this book. Whether you are studying, working for an organisation or working for yourself you will find that your communication can be improved if you respect these key ideas and be aware of them whenever you communicate.

Before leaving this section let's summarise these key questions in a form of a checklist.

Checklist

- Is this communication necessary?   ❏
- Is it targeted?   ❏
- Is it timely?   ❏
- Is it in the right language?   ❏
- Is it clear?   ❏
- Is it accurate?   ❏
- Is it short and to the point?   ❏
- Does it cover what it should cover?   ❏
- Can we get a response?   ❏
- Is the tone OK? Adult not parental   ❏

We hope that you have found and will continue to find this book helpful in enhancing your communication skills and so your careers whether these be vertical, horizontal, portfolio in shape, or a combination of all three!

General Reading on Communications

S Adams, The Dilbert Principle, Boxtree, 1997. It's not just the cartoons but the wonderful e-mailed examples of appalling communications from readers which make this such a stimulating text.

M Argyle, The Psychology of Interpersonal Behaviour, Penguin, 1992. A ground breaking book which through its many editions has had a tremendous impact on how we think of communications.

E Goffman, The Presentation of Self in Everyday Life, Penguin, 1974. Another landmark in the interpretation of inter personal communications. Particularly interesting examples.

J Honey, DoesAccent Matter?, Faber, 1992. A stimulating text. Do may not agree with Honey but he will make you think.

U Markham, How to Deal with Dificult People, Thorsons Business, 1998. A very useful book full of practical advice.

D Rowntree, The Manager's Book of Checklists, Corgi, 1991. A useful set of checklists, many of which are directly concerned with communications.

R Semler, Maverick, Arrow, 1994. This is about business and a revolutionary way of running an organisation; it is full of implications for how to stimulate communication between the different layers.